Geoff: 44 years a railwayman

By L. Geoffrey Raynor

First published by Plowright Press 2000

British Library Cataloguing in Publication Data
A catalogue record for this book is available from the British Library

ISBN 0 9516960 6 8

PLOWRIGHT PRESS
P O BOX 66
WARWICK CV34 4XE

Orders from Plowright Press (£9.95 plus £1.50 p & p UK) or through a bookseller

Printer: Warwick Printing Company Ltd, Warwick

CONTENTS Page

EDITOR'S FOREWORD

Geoff Raynor's personal history is a vital record in two respects. First, he presents an insider's view of what was a British institution of the second half of the 20th century, British Railways (later British Rail). His railway career of 44 years was virtually as long as the lifetime of BR, the nationalised service which existed from 1948 to November 1997 when its last train, a freight train, ran.

Second, his history is, of course, unique to him, as all our histories are uniquely our own. His experience of events and therefore his memories could never be exactly the same as anybody else's. However, those memories can be shared, by being told, and that is what Geoff has done. As he sums it up: 'It's fact, truth, and how our lives were.'

Thanks: I would like to thank the following for their friendly, interested and generous help:

Anchorage School; Don Baker; British Railways Board Records Office; Burma Star Association; Department for Education and Employment; Doncaster Archives; Doncaster Reference Library; Drax power station; EWS Railway; Vincent Kelly; Leamington Spa Library; Lincoln and Louth NHS Trust; Mansfield Local Studies Library; Myanmar Embassy; North Nottinghamshire Health Authority; Nottinghamshire Archives; Nottingham Local Studies Library; Nottingham Library; Alan Pegler; Peterborough Local Studies Library; John Marrs, Editor, Peterborough Post and Herald; Rossington Pheasant Bank Junior School, Doncaster; Rotherham Archives; Rotherham Local Studies; Sheffield Local Studies Library; St George's Hospital, Lincoln; Peter Walton. The BR material is used with kind permission of the British Railways Board.

Anne Bott, Warwick, 2000

The author Geoff Raynor, in 1999.

INTRODUCTION

In 1983 I retired from British Rail after 44 years of continuous service on the Railways. My wife, Janet, meanwhile was still teaching at Anchorage, a Special School in Doncaster, and continued to be the Deputy Head, a position which she had held from 1972.

Being retired was to me at that time quite a big change and, although I did the housework and cooking, etc, I found time on my hands. I have never found household jobs boring, and one can think when one is vacuuming a room.

It was whilst doing the vacuuming in fact that I first decided to put my life story on paper. I therefore began to write about the things that had taken place during the time up to and including 1983.

Although I wrote quite a few chapters, other things occurred and it was not until 1998 that I decided finally to finish the story. I wanted to do so before Janet died. We were always aware that she might not live for long.

Janet died of breast cancer in March 1999, after fighting the disease for more than 30 years. When I was writing my story, she said: "Don't put anything down about me." Now I can give an account of her life, of her courage and willpower, and this I have added at the end of the book.

I trust that readers will enjoy the history of the Railways as I experienced them 1939 to 1983; also the events following retirement.

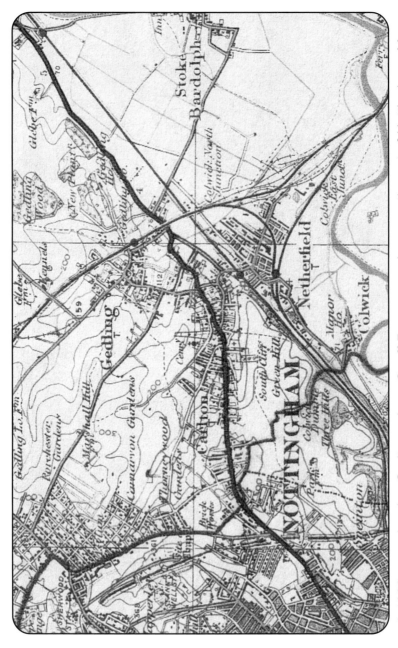

A 1932 map showing Carlton, where Geoff Raynor was born, north-east of Nottingham. Map reproduced by kind permission of Ordnance Survey and Nottingham Local Studies Library.

1. IN THE BEGINNING AT CARLTON

I was born on 22nd August, 1922, at Carlton, a suburban area on the outskirts of Nottingham, being the third child of my parents; the eldest, Gertrude, was six years of age, the second child, William, two years and four months at this time.

Both Gertrude and William were bright children. I, on the other hand, had much to do to keep up with my peers at School. This I was able to do, despite suffering a fractured skull when I was nine years of age in a road accident.

Whilst playing with other, older children I was knocked down by a lorry which had taken miners to Gedling Colliery and was travelling back towards Nottingham empty. I ran behind a stationary tram and then out into the path of the lorry, which was passing the tram.

The accident occurred on 8th December, 1931, which meant that I spent Christmas in Nottingham General Hospital.

It was whilst I was in Hospital that I found out that Santa Claus was only a myth. I happened to be awake when the Nurses brought the presents round the ward; lucky for me I had the good sense to pretend that I was still asleep and eyed my presents with joy.

They were in a very large sack of muslin or suchlike material and the sack looked to be full, as indeed I found it to be when I opened it later on Christmas morning. There were toys, books, pencils, paints, etc.

I had nine months off School due to the accident, including five weeks in Hospital in bed, not allowed to put my feet on the floor at

No. 53 Mayfield Road, Carlton, where Geoff was born (above), and No. 43 Mayfield Road (left) where he and his family lived from 1925.

Photos taken by the author, 1999.

4

all. To be on your own all day when everyone else was at School made life lonely.

I tried to find things to do. I ran errands for neighbours. I collected eggs for one, for which I got an egg. I turned the mangle for another, for which I was given a penny (an old penny, less than 1/2p in today's money); I rather think this was to get rid of me. The rest of the time I just messed about.

It will be of no surprise to learn that my mother, Alice, became fed up with me being always 'under my feet', as she called it. She therefore arranged for me to go back to School before the Hospital Doctor approved.

I attended an Elementary School about a mile away from home, as did my brother and sister; its name was Porchester Senior Mixed Council School and it was at the other end of Standhill Road. Before that, until the spring of 1931, I was at Porchester Junior School, also in Standhill Road but just round the corner from my home in Mayfield Road.

Bill and I very often walked to School together; Gertrude, being older, had already left when I joined the Senior School, but she would have walked with other girls, not us.

Examinations were held at the Senior School each year for the brightest children to go to a Grammar School; my sister and brother should have sat this examination but, as my parents could not afford to buy the School Uniform to clothe either of them, neither did – that they could have passed it I do not doubt.

My sister worked as a Clerk in the offices of Boots' Cash Chemist, then left in 1940 to be a Clerk at the Trustee Savings Bank, eventually becoming a Relief Bank Manager and travelling to TSB branches in the outlying areas of Nottingham. My brother never had other than first-class grades and more often than not took honours when exams were done. I, of course, was not allowed to take homework home as it was considered too much for me after my accident and therefore I had no chance of sitting the exam. Those taking the Grammar School exam were given homework beforehand.

My father, George Lewis, was a Master Painter, and he had a knowledge of sign-writing, gilding and all that sort of thing. In the First World War he was in the Sherwood Foresters, then pontoon building, then the Tank Corps, then on the Physical Training Staff at the Army's Aldershot HQ as a Drill Instructor, a Sergeant.

He was a Foreman Painter for a firm of private and commercial decorators named Riley's, but every year as I remember he was out of work about Christmas time; things picked up towards the end of February when people began to want their spring cleaning done.

In 1937, when he was 48 years old, my father was found to have TB, as consumption was known in those days; he therefore had to go into a tuberculosis sanatorium run by the County Council at Rainworth near Mansfield, Ransom Sanatorium it was called, staying there for six months.

This was a big blow to our family and the lack of money was always with us; the sick pay from his Trade Union was almost negligible. My mother took washing in at one time, whilst Bill and I had paper rounds.

How we managed I never knew – my mother did her best under terrible conditions and kept us well fed. She was a first-class cook and mostly won the cake competition organised by the ladies at the Methodist Church in Standhill Road; she had very strong wrists, which gave her a great advantage when it came to beating the eggs and so forth.

Both my mother and father were members of the Methodist Church.

6

They had been brought up at Basford, a suburb of Nottingham, my mother's father being a Policeman and my father's father being a Plasterer. They all attended Sherwood Methodist Church.

At Carlton services were held in the Senior School where we attended Day School. Later, when I was about 15, a plot of land was bought in Standhill Road and a wooden hut placed on the land and services were then held in this.

It was also used for social evenings every Saturday in the Winter months – I met my wife, Janet, there when I was 18 and she was 16 – as well as other meetings.

Eventually, a proper brick building was erected at the side of it. When the new Church was built, the wooden hut became the School room.

The wooden hut used as a church and for socials, at one of which Geoff and Janet met, on 21 September 1940. Photo taken by the author, 1999.

St Nicholas' Choir, about 1934. The Rector, Rev S Metcalfe, is in the middle, second row, with choirmaster Mr Keefe on his left, organist Ray Smith on his right. Bill is sixth from the right, Geoff fourth from the right, both front row. Roller-skating Stan is first left, second row; herb-smoking Riley is second left, front row (see chapter 3).

8

2. DEATH AT 1177 YEARS

At the age of 10 my brother Bill, as we called him, joined the Choir of St Nicholas' Church at Castle Gate which, as its name suggests, is near where Nottingham Castle is situated (the tower of this Church was used by Cavaliers to fire on the Castle where the Roundheads were in position during the Civil War).

It was a very old Church and I kept on to my mother to let me join the Choir, which she was loath to do. She didn't like me being out of her sight following my head injury; I was known as accident-prone after that.

However, when I was 10 years of age she relented and I accompanied Bill to join the Choir, after being given strict instructions as to what we should and should not do. For instance, we must behave ourselves when travelling on the bus, and we must travel straight home afterwards, not play about.

I enjoyed the position as Choirboy, especially as it was a good Choir; it was composed of 22 lads, nine women and about 12 men. We did cantatas and other pieces by notable Composers, eg Bach.

Choir practice was held on Wednesdays and Fridays in the Church. On Wednesdays we trained alone, no adults. On Fridays the adults joined us at about 7 pm; we had to start at 6 o'clock or 6.30 pm.

Mr Keefe was the Choirmaster; he had been a Teacher at the Sunday School at Sherwood Methodist Church where my mother and father had attended and this, of course, made it easy for us to join St Nicholas' Choir. In any case, boy Choir members were always in demand in most C of E Churches.

I can still see Mr Keefe tapping out the time with his pencil and woe betide any boy who did not keep time or tone. He would stop the Choir and the person or persons responsible were immediately taken to task for their failure. He always had the power to fine you if he thought this would make you do better.

He fined one boy for drawing during the sermon. The drawings were all characters in the Choir, wonderfully done in the vein of cartoons The Choirmaster confiscated them – then had them mounted in a picture frame and hung in his own home.

The Choirboys would meet at the large iron gate which led to the door of the Church down a pathway flanked by graves; during Winter nights no-one dared to go down there alone.

On one occasion I remember a group of boys were preparing to go down the pathway to Choir practice. It was a cold Winter's night; a gas lamp outside the gate was the only means of light. Then, as we passed through the gate, we noticed two white hands moving from the Church towards us – we all shouted in fright and took to our heels through the gate and up the road.

When we came to our senses we turned round and looked back, noticing as we did so that the hands we had seen coming from the Church belonged to a Policeman who had evidently been having a crafty smoke in the Church doorway and, having finished, put his white gloves on again.

It was never pleasant walking down this pathway in the dark. Most of the graves beside it were very old; one was marked that the person lying there was, if I remember rightly, 177 years of age when he died. Although the Records of the Church were searched no-one was able to confirm or deny this remarkable age.

Of course, this did not stop the Choirboys from scratching another '1' in front of the figures, making it read 1177 years.

No-one owned up to making this mark so all the boys were fined sixpence, or 6d (21/2p); this Mr Keefe was able to do as each boy was paid one penny per attendance. It cost Bill and I a half-penny each to ride on the trolley-bus into town from Carlton, about three miles (nearly 5 km) away to the North-east, and a half-penny back.

The worst thing I remember was to want to go to the toilet whilst a service was taking place – I have known boys collapse under the strain. I never passed out but it was the one thing I feared during a service. It was also difficult as there were no toilets to use; one had to go behind gravestones to relieve oneself.

St Nicholas' Church with (foreground) the gas lamp which lit such a small area that walking towards the church meant going into darkness. Photo by kind permission of Nottingham Local Studies Library.

*Choirboys
Bill (left)
and Geoff,
1933.*

3. ANGELS – AND MISCHIEF-MAKERS

Most of the boys were older than I and when in song looked and sounded like angels but outside the Church reverted to what all boys do, ie mischief.

Stan, one of the top boys who took solos, used to have one roller-skate which he wore on his right foot; I have known him to get on the trolley-bus at the same stop as Bill and I and clamber up the stairs, making a great clatter as he did so, and when the Conductor came up the stairs, Stan was smoking a cigarette and tendered the half-fare.

This infuriated the Conductor who told Stan to either put out the cigarette or pay the full adult fare, which you had to do when you reached 14 years of age.

Stan made a great thing of stubbing out the cigarette, and relit the stub when the Conductor had gone down the stairs.

On his one roller-skate Stan would make for the Council House, of which Nottingham is justly proud; it is a very fine building. He would go along the centre of the sloping walkway which passes through the Council House, dodging all the people as they made their way home, squatting down as he travelled at speed.

On one occasion I remember him travelling down the slope when a Policeman came walking by. With Stan travelling straight in front of him, the Policeman gave chase but could not catch him.

Another boy, named Riley (no relation of the people my father worked for), smoked a pipe filled with herbs, anything he could get, cloves etc; it smelt awful but he kept smoking it. One boy was sacked for throwing a demoncracker into the Chancel whilst the choir was in full song. This was a thin type of firework, only about two and a half inches (64 mm) long, but it made a tremendous bang when lit, especially in a place like a Chancel.

Other times I remember we played football in the square known as 'Slab Square' which lies directly in front of the Council House. This square, the old Market Square, is of concrete and was just the thing for being able to knock a ball about.

Nottingham City Police did not think so, however, and, as I was mostly in goal and first saw the Policeman approach, the others would hear me shout and see me running and know they had to get away as fast as possible – and they would then all run in different directions.

When on our way to and from the Church we would often stop and listen to the speakers who were in 'Slab Square' on Fridays and Sundays.

We listened to the Communists, Irish Republicans (Green shirts), Blackshirts (Oswald Mosley's Fascists). The Salvation Army too were there, and Church dignitaries, including Bishop Neville Talbot, a respected Church leader who had resigned his see in Pretoria to become Vicar of St Mary's in Nottingham. In the First World War he had been behind the setting-up of the original Toc H club in Belgium for soldiers fighting at Ypres, six miles away.

A nondescript person we knew as Bergoine used to address the public, usually on a soapbox, giving his political views. On one occasion, calling the Nottingham City Fathers for all he was worth, he said: "If I were the Lord Mayor of Nottingham . . . "

At this point some wag in the audience shouted: "I'd have overhead sewers." This caused such a lot of merriment that poor old Bergoine had great difficulty in getting back to his theme; whether he ever made it I don't know as we had to leave before this could occur.

Although we had a good Choir, as I have already stated, I cannot in truth say that I had ever seen the Church full and it was not until 1978, years later, that I did see it absolutely full for a service, when I accompanied my son, who was doing a postgraduate course at Nottingham University.

Apparently all the declared Christians who attended the University came to worship at the Church of St Nicholas and it was a very evangelical assembly of those who have declared to the community that they are followers of Jesus Christ.

The Council House, Nottingham, 'Slab Square' in the foreground. Photo taken by the author, 1999.

4. HERO LARWOOD HOME

About the time I was a choirboy Nottinghamshire had a great cricketing side.

Larwood, Voce, Hardstaff and Lilley (wicket-keeper) were the heroes and I remember quite clearly being taken by my father to the Midland Station at Nottingham one night, along with the other enthusiasts, to see Harold Larwood come back from the Ashes series of 1932-33 in Australia, where a political storm had just been averted following the leg-theory incidents, or body-line bowling as the Australians called it.

Larwood had some foot problem, having bowled cricket balls at 100 miles per hour at Australian cricketers on the hard Australian wickets.

Of course, all Nottingham were very partisan in respect of their hero and this resulted in thousands moving towards the station, now the city's only Railway Station. I remember travelling from the old Market Square holding my father's hand and holding on to his coat belt, my feet never touching the ground en route.

Looking back now, it seems quite crazy to have done this, but the Police managed to get Larwood away without the crowd being aware of it until he was well clear of the station, the crowd being good-humoured. Then they dispersed, singing and shouting.

Another thing I remember when I was young and Australia were playing England here in England was that my father took Bill and I to 'Slab Square' adjacent to the Council House where hundreds of people had gathered, looking across towards Friar Lane where, at one time, at the top of a high building a large notice was displayed which read, "Ino' Flakes wash everything.'

This notice was lit up at night but, on this occasion, a large green board with a wooden surround, like a billiard table, had been placed at this point. Two wickets were placed upon it and a red ball could be seen to move to where the English or Australian either hit or missed it.

If the ball stopped at the wicket, this was another wicket taken. I don't know the date when this took place or how it was done but it was some years before the Second World War.

Looking towards Friar Lane from the Council House, to the high building in the background, site of the 'Ino Flakes' notice. Photo taken in 1999 by the author.

Bill (left) and Geoff on holiday in the late 1930s in Skegness, where they were staying at their aunt's guesthouse. Bill was 18 years old and Geoff was 16.

5. AT WORK AT VIYELLA HOUSE

Bill should have left School when he was 14 years old, the age to leave Elementary School. However, just before he was due to leave, my father happened to be working at the house of a high-ranking official of Messrs John Player and Son, the well-known cigarette manufacturer which was in Radford.

My father came to an understanding with this person, who proposed that Bill should stay at School until he was 15, when he would be able to apply for a job in the offices of Player. This was done with the special permission of the Head Master of Porchester Senior Mixed Council School, where we were educated.

However, when the day of reckoning arrived, the high official didn't want to know, saying there were no vacancies. Bill therefore had been kept at School a year longer than he should have been, a great sacrifice by my parents, and to be thrown on to the market at 15 when other children had left at 14 was also a blow.

He finally got a job with Messrs William Hollins and Co, Castle Boulevard, Nottingham, most famous for their Viyella range, who made shirts, pyjamas, ladies' and children's underwear, and also piece goods (lengths of cloth, in a roll or wrapped round a wooden board).

I followed Bill there when I left School at 14. Actually, when I left at the end of the Summer term I was 13 years, 11 months and one week old and therefore had to wait about three weeks until my birthday before I could start work.

Bill was in the offices and I went into the pattern room. There I sneezed continually, caused by the fluff and dust from making up patterns of cloth into pattern books, tailors' samples etc, and this to me was terrible. I later discovered that I was allergic to cloth!

Eventually I moved to the mail room where I found I worked about an hour's overtime each day. At the end of the day all the letters, pamphlets, promotions, etc, had to be collated, stamped or franked. Very often it required longer than our laid-down hours of work to get all these ready for the Post Office.

The pay was very poor at Messrs William Hollins, especially for men who worked in the offices and were on a basic wage.

It was the practice at this firm to take trainees (most of these were from Public Schools) and they were guaranteed a Sales Representative's position at the end of their time, which they spent in various offices, workshops, etc. Before the Second World War a Representative's position was considered a very good job and the Reps were well remunerated, being paid on sales and getting bonuses.

Some were nice fellows but these were few and far between; most had wealthy fathers and were snobs and would not have stood a chance on the open labour market. Their fathers had bought them a position with the firm and some of these trainees were absolute 'Charlies'.

As one who had little to help him other than his own brain, Bill went to Night School, as indeed did I. We were encouraged to do so by the firm, although I can't remember William Hollins paying any of the fees. We had to pay our own.

Subjects we took included the theory and practice of Commerce, and English; Bill also took Shorthand and I took Maths. We studied at the Cottesmore Evening Institute, held in Cottesmore School, Lenton Boulevard, and at the Huntingdon Evening Institute, which was held in Huntingdon School, Huntingdon Street. Bill also took a more advanced course, in Textiles, run by Nottingham University College, as Nottingham University was then known, at their buildings in Shakespeare Street.

After each year of study, an examination was held and on three occasions Bill was awarded a prize. They were book prizes, all on Textiles.

For all this, William Hollins told him to look for another job; he had got to an age when they would have had to pay him more. A number of firms did this.

His call-up papers arrived at about this time in 1939 and he went into the Royal Corps of Signals. In six months he was sent to Singapore, having obtained 98% in his course on Wireless and its operation.

Looking back, it seems ridiculous that in 1938, at the start of the Munich crisis, a Territorial Army squad of about five men were deployed on the roof of Viyella House, where William Hollins had its offices and warehouse.

These men were equipped with a Bren gun which was positioned on the flat roof and was to be used against aircraft; they wouldn't have stood a chance if there really had been German bombers sent over, not with one machine-gun. The squad was subsequently withdrawn when the Munich crisis ended.

6. BEHIND THE LINES AT NOTTINGHAM VICTORIA STATION

On 14th August, 1939, I left William Hollins and joined the London and North Eastern Railway at Nottingham Victoria Station as Messenger Boy to the District Superintendent, having been dissatisfied at William Hollins with little or no prospects.

I made valiant efforts to get a job on the Railways; a Driver's job appealed to me at that time. On the off-chance I wrote applying for entrance as a Cleaner at the LNER Colwick Locomotive Depot which was East of the city centre; this would have involved cleaning steam engines, including the firebox and smokebox, oiling, and preparing the fire in the firebox. It was the first step to becoming a Driver.

The Depot Master told me by letter that I was too young, as it was a Company rule I had to be 17 years of age before I could be taken on. However, he could offer me a job as an Apprentice Fitter in the Maintenance Depot. This did not appeal to me, so I went for a position of Van Lad at the London, Midland and Scottish Railway Goods Depot on Station Street, but found they had no vacancies.

I then decided to apply at the District Superintendent's Office at Victoria Station on the last day of my leave from William Hollins. I therefore went to the Staff Office, which was part of the District Superintendent's Office and was on No. 1 platform at Victoria Station.

On knocking on the door, I was told: "Come in." On entering the office I saw a man dressed in a dark suit, wearing spectacles and bending over his desk, apparently writing something. When he looked up I saw he had a little moustache.

I found out later that this was Mr Searson, Assistant to the Chief Clerk. His first question was: "What do you want?" I quickly told him that I was desirous of joining the Railway Company and of my efforts to obtain a job at Colwick Locomotive Depot and also with the LMS Goods Depot, without success.

From then on he wrote all my answers to his questions on a form and at the end spoke into his telephone. Then he turned to me, took his pocket-watch out, looked at me and said: "Can you be at the Medical Office at London Road Low Level in 10 minutes?"

I gave this assurance, knowing that it was a good half-hour's walk to this station South of the city and I would have to run all the way. This I did, dodging through the crowds of people shopping, avoiding cars and lorries, and arriving breathless at the Medical Office.

I was there within the time, so demonstrating that I wanted the job badly enough. However, it was not until some three-quarters of an hour later that the Medical Officer saw me.

There were about 20 or 30 other men there, Drivers, Guards, Signalmen; all had to have medical examinations on the basis of one, two, three or more years' service. Eyesight and physical fitness were paramount.

The Medical Officer gave me a physical and eyesight test. He seemed satisfied that I was all in one piece and then told me to return to the Victoria Station Staff Office and he would advise Mr Searson of his findings. On arriving back at the Staff Office I was told that I had passed the tests and I would be taken on. "When can you start?"

I said that I would have to give a week's notice and would be able to start on 14th August. The wage I was receiving at William Hollins and Co was 12/6d (62½p) per week. I was to start on the Railway at £1, clearly a big jump. My parents were very pleased with me and thought that I should have a good living in front of me, as had other relatives of the family who had been on the Railway for some considerable time. My mother's eldest sister had married an LNER Driver and her son was a Fireman.

Mr Searson had asked whether I had relatives on the Railway and I had said: "No", as they were not near family and we only had a distant sort of relationship. This had seemed to please him but I do not know why.

It goes to show that it's a matter of luck how one answers questions at an interview. If I had told the truth I suppose I should not have got the job and I found out later that Railways usually were very much a family job concern, with father, son and grandson being employed by the Companies.

Nottingham Victoria Station in LNER days, taken from Mansfield Road. The clock tower is all that remains of the station. Photo by kind permission of Nottingham Local Studies Library.

24

7. MESSENGER BOY

On the morning of 14th August, 1939, I reported to the District Superintendent's Office at 8 o'clock; my hours were to be 8 am to 5.30 pm, or until completion of work, Monday to Friday, 8 am to 12.30 pm Saturdays.

The job entailed opening correspondence from stations and members of the public, and distributing these to the various offices – Passenger, Freight, General and Staff offices; then the Management had their own offices. I also collected letters from these offices and despatched them to their addresses.

I had to meet trains for urgent letters and deliver them to their respective destinations in the Superintendent's office. Urgent letters could be time sheets, accident reports, Witnesses' statements, complaints from members of the public, Police reports.

During the afternoon, I had a large amount of correspondence to despatch; after-hours working depended on the amount and on whether the District Superintendent or other Management had signed their letters. I had to wait until this was done, so that I could despatch them.

Saturday was the worst day as the District Superintendent and the Goods Manager went into the Victoria Station Hotel for a drink before signing their letters. No overtime was paid.

I also had to run off typed circulars on the Gestetner machine. This was a machine on which typed 'skins' were placed. Ink was then placed on the skin by a roller, after which the handle of the machine had to be turned, which printed the skins' typed matter on to waiting paper. This was done in co-operation with two other youths who belonged to the Goods Manager's Organisation.

These two were at times most unco-operative youths; however, I soon learned to deal with them for my own ends. There were several things I could do, no co-operation for one, which tended to even things up.

On 3rd September war between Great Britain and Germany was declared. I had been ordered to be at work, on overtime, and it was the first time I had ever worked on a Sunday.

I was to run off on the Gestetner machine certain circulars which transpired to be instructions for issue to stations and depots cancelling the working time-table and instituting a war time-table. These circulars had to be sent out immediately they were printed and checked.

What surprised me was that no-one knew war was to be declared but that provision had been made by the Railways for the Staff to be brought in for this duty. No explanation had been given for Staff to come to work specially.

It was not until just before 12 o'clock that news came through concerning the war having been declared. In those days there was no television, only the radio, which was not the technical piece of equipment we are used to today.

Newspapers were brought out specially and brought on to the streets; the men selling them would shout: "Special" for all their worth and people would then buy a paper for the price of one penny.

Incidentally, cigarettes were 6d for 10 Player's. From a vending machine against a wall of the station building one could get a carton of two Plus-Two cigarettes and one match for 1d and I have often done so – they were not a bad smoke either.

The night war broke out the sirens sounded for the first time; all the members of our family came downstairs and we all looked out of the front room window. There was a bright, full moon and we looked for we knew not what. It so happened that it was a false alarm and we then made our way back to bed.

A self-portrait of Geoff in railway uniform, with Bennie, the family's dog, about 1940.

8. LOOKING FOR SABOTEURS

About the time of Dunkirk, Anthony Eden, who became Foreign Secretary in Churchill's Cabinet, asked for men to join the Local Defence Volunteers, as the Home Guard was known at first, and I, with so many other Railway workers, joined the Railway Battalion within the Home Guard.

We walked round Victoria Station looking for saboteurs and trespassers. The patrol of the station area was done in two shifts during the night period with, as far as I remember, the first two men starting at 10 pm and finishing at midnight; the next two men midnight until 1 am; the first two men 1 am to 2 am; the second two men 2 am to 4 am, and the first two men 4 am to 6 am, when the patrol stood down. The NCO stayed in the Guard Room.

Victoria Station was in the centre of Nottingham. To build the Railway here the Engineers had to cut through rock, thus the station was a balloon type with tunnels, Mansfield Road and Victoria Street tunnels, at each end. The station had a glass roof.

Twice per week we were on duty and we had to walk round the station area, tunnel to tunnel, end to end over the metals, ie rails, etc, also the Goods and Platform areas.

At first, as is well known, we didn't have rifles and it was not until some considerable time after the patrols were in operation that we were given Canadian Ross Rifles. Even then they were First World War rifles which had been stored by the Canadians in tunnels, caves, etc.

We were given a machine-gun and hand grenades. These were

locked in a cupboard, the Sergeant in charge having the key, and the only time we unlocked this cupboard was one particular night when on standby in the Guard Room. Jerry planes were passing overhead at high altitude – the glass of Victoria Station roof must have given Jerry every assistance.

Soldiers with anti-aircraft guns at Colwick Woods were firing at the planes, loud reports being heard as they did so. The Sergeant, myself and another member of our group left the Guard Room to view the spectacle, the first patrol being in the station area.

We all noticed round circles in the sky drifting towards the earth and we were certain these were parachutists. The Sergeant therefore rang the Major (a District Inspector) at his home and he flatly refused to come out or do anything.

Therefore we trotted out the machine-gun with all available ammunition etc and stood to all night; however, it appears that what we had seen was the smoke from the anti-aircraft shells after they had exploded. Had there been parachutists, I don't know what the result would have been.

There were some narrow escapes when carrying out patrols, as locomotive and train movements continued all the while; locomotives emitted spouts of steam and smoke to high heaven that made visibility very difficult, and there was also the noise, such noise. High-visibility vests, which now have to be worn by Staff on the track, were not thought of.

One had to cross over the Railway tracks where the movements were taking place and there were several separate lines to negotiate: Goods lines, Main lines and Shunt lines, Loop lines, Up lines (ie those going towards London) and Down lines. Sets of tracks had to be crossed, the rails being 4 feet 81/2 inches (or 1.4351 m) apart, as well as the 6 feet space between the sets. The rails were laid on stone ballast.

It was very difficult to make quick progress when on patrol. I remember I was just about to cross from the Down Goods line to the Down Loop line in fog one night when, for some reason, I took my foot off the rail and stood for about one second.

Just then the front buffer beam of a locomotive, travelling in reverse, passed me on the Loop line; my knee was nearly under the buffer beam. This was one of the closest shaves I had on the line.

Another self-portrait, this time of Geoff as defence volunteer in 1940. He joined the Local Defence Volunteers, subsequently renamed the Home Guard.

9. SAFETY IN EAST LEAKE

About six months after joining the Railway Company, I was instructed to go as Messenger Boy to East Leake, about eight miles South of Nottingham, towards Loughborough, in a country area.

An air raid shelter had been built for the Control, Freight and Passenger Trains offices to be located there for the duration of the war.

All the shutters for the windows of this air raid shelter were made of three-quarter-inch battleship steel and needed two men to move them into position. I did this once with another person and that was enough for me; we each had to put one foot on the wall of the shelter to get them to move.

Life at East Leake was great – I enjoyed every minute I was there. I used to catch the train at 8 o'clock in the morning from Victoria Station, having first obtained the correspondence and mail that was to be sorted for the various offices.

I did this on the train and, on arriving at East Leake, I collected some more correspondence etc and took the lot to the air raid shelter. There I did further sorting and then distributed the letters to the offices, placing these on the desks of the Clerks to whom they were addressed.

The first time I went to East Leake I found that in the Main General Office, which was a large rectangular room, the concrete ceiling was half an inch thick with ice. It was perishing.

Two fires burned, one each end of the room, glowing with hot coals, and each of the Clerks – there were about 10 of them, male and female – had a lighted paraffin stove heater at the side of their desks. Drops of water spattered everywhere from the melting ice.

I, of course, was not given a heater. It was not too bad in the Control Room, but this office was open continuously.

Geoff's parents and his sister,
Gertrude, in the summer of 1940.

After about three months I was sent back to Nottingham; I had gone to East Leake to cover a vacancy and another boy had been appointed and trained for the job.

I applied for a position as Train Register Boy (or Lad) at Victoria North signal box and was given the job. This was promotion.

I had been told by Mr Searson, Assistant to the Chief Clerk, that I was to become a Signalman and so that ended the matter. I could not apply to be a Driver; he was acknowledging no more applications to become Cleaners/Drivers.

Four signal boxes were located within the station area and the South box was actually just beneath Parliament Street Bridge. The East box, if I remember rightly, was situated between platforms 7 and 10, and West box was between Nos. 1 and 4 platforms.

The North box was about 70 yards (or 64 m) South of Mansfield Road tunnel which we always called Carrington tunnel, Carrington Station having been next along the line. There were two turntables provided, at the North and South ends of the station.

The duties I had to perform as a TR Boy were to record all train movements at the North end of the station, answer calls on the two telephones – one connected to Control, the other to local signal boxes – pass messages to other signal boxes and keep Control informed of train delays etc. I was given training in the signal box before starting.

The employment of TR Boys depended on the number of train

Left and below left: signalling a train, involving block instruments (Regulations for Train Signalling and Signalmen's General Instructions, BR 29960, October 1972, pp. 8-9).

Below: block instrument showing the three indicator positions, Train on line, Line clear and Line blocked (photo by the author, 2000).

REGULATIONS

1. MODE OF SIGNALLING

"A", "B" and "C" represent three consecutive signal boxes, and the process of signalling a train is as follows:—

(a) Prior to the despatch of a train from "A" the Signalman there, provided he has received the **Train out of section** signal for the previous train and the block indicator is in the normal position, must call the attention of "B", and having obtained it, send the proper **Is line clear** signal. If the line is clear at "B" the Signalman there may acknowledge the signal and place the block indicator to the **Line clear** position.

Regulations for train signalling on double lines by the absolute block system—*continued*

1. Mode of Signalling—*continued*

(b) The Signalman at "A" may then, if the line is clear, clear his signals for the train to leave "A".

(c) On the train leaving "A" the Signalman there must send the **Train entering section** signal to "B", and the Signalman at "B" must acknowledge the signal and place the block indicator to the **Train on line** position.

(d) "B" must then, provided he has received the **Train out of section** signal for the previous train, and the block indicator is in the normal position, call the attention of "C", and having obtained it, must send the proper **Is line clear** signal to "C". On receiving permission from "C" for the train to approach, "B" may clear his signals for the train to proceed to "C", and when the train has arrived at or passed "B" or has been shunted clear of the line at "B", the Signalman there must call the attention of "A" and, having obtained it, send the **Train out of section** signal, which signal must be acknowledged, and place or maintain the block indicator at the normal position.

(e) Where special authority has been given in order to avoid delay to the train, the **Is line clear** signal must be sent forward as soon as the **Is line clear** signal has been acknowledged and before the **Train entering section** signal has been received from the box in rear, when this can be done in accordance with the Regulations under which the **Is line clear** signal may be sent.

(f) Where it is necessary that a Signalman who has acknowledged the **Is line clear** signal for a train should receive an intimation of its approach before it enters the section, the **Train approaching** signal (1–2–1) must, where authorised, be sent in accordance with the special instructions issued.

movements at stations or junctions. Signalmen, who received pay on a points system, were given so many points for having a TR Boy.

Numerous train movements were made at the North signal box. There were through passenger trains, and local and long-distance trains. Some passenger trains conveyed vans and so forth at the rear of the passenger compartments.

The station shunter (locomotive) took these vans etc and placed them where they could be offloaded or placed on the rear of another train. In the Dock area Messrs Player & Sons, cigarette manufacturers, and other firms worked on vans which would be attached to the rear of passenger trains.

The acceptance of trains, arrivals and departures, shunting movements, all had to be recorded in a book and the time noted. Therefore the clock in the signal box had to be accurate and a time check was given on the phone by the station Telegraph Office each day at 10 am precisely; the bell rang for a full minute.

There were many phone calls. Control, out at East Leake in the air raid shelter, was where co-ordination of Railway Services was made, and that office, as well as other signal boxes, used the telephone to ascertain where trains were etc. The TR Boy had to give Control and other signal boxes notice of train arrivals and departures.

TR Boys were not supposed to work the signals or points or answer the Block Instruments, the means by which trains were accepted and passed on to other signal boxes.

This was done by Bell Signalling and an instrument showing three positions: 'Line clear', 'Train on line' and 'Line blocked' (this last was the normal position). The line was considered blocked to other trains until acceptance of the train in question was given by repeating the recognised Bell signal, ie four beats on the Bell indicated an express passenger train was being offered. However, as I became more conversant with the Block Instruments and lever frame (where the levers were connected to points, lock bars and signals), the Signalman would let me answer the Block Bells and move the levers whilst he had a cup of tea and a bite to eat.

We TR Boys worked a two-shift system, 6 am to 2 pm and 2 pm to 10 pm. The Signalmen worked a three-shift system to enable the box to be open continuously and their extra shift was 10 pm to 6 am.

Located within the Victoria North signal box were two steel cabinets or shelters, one for the Signalman and the other for the TR Boy to take refuge in during air raids; each cabinet had a door and the top was also hinged. That worried me; I thought any blast would push me through the top.

The cabinets were to protect the signal box Staff from flying glass; signal boxes at this time were built with glass windows on all four sides.

It should be noted that today's power boxes, which superseded signal boxes and, indeed, took over the areas of a number of them in various places, are very different; they have brick walls with small windows and the insides are illuminated by strip lighting. Signals and lines are also illuminated: signals are red, yellow or green, depending on whether they are being operated, whilst lines are white when not occupied and majenta when a train is travelling over them.

I remember when an air raid was in progress on one occasion, some time between 7.30 and 9 o'clock one night; the anti-aircraft guns were at their height and bombs were falling. Bill, the Signalman, was in his shelter and I in mine when the Block Bell rang. Bill shouted to me to answer the Bell – I hesitated and then went to answer it, Bill telling me to accept the train being offered, which I did.

Most of the worst raids on Nottingham, however, took place when Arthur was on nights. He seemed to always fall for it. He was a lovely chap and proudly told me he was a Methodist.

His son was at this time about 24 years of age but as a young boy had gone to the swimming baths, where some youths had thrown him in and had broken his back, causing him to be a cripple for the rest of his life. I never knew Arthur to complain and he was always cheerful.

Sammy was the other regular Signalman. He was small, about five feet in height, and was the image of Hitler. It was his habit to wear a tam-o'-shanter at work which was brown in colour.

It was also his practice to wave to the trains for Derby (and others if he spotted them) as they left No. 3 bay, the non-through train platform which was nearest the signal box. One female, who regularly travelled on this, gave him a white tam-o'-shanter, which he wore only on special occasions.

He swore like a trooper and fairly raced along the frame; one soon learned to keep out of Sammy's way or get knocked flying.

Signals, &c. not to be worked by unauthorised persons. **71.** (*a*) Train Register Boys, or other unauthorised persons must not be allowed to work signals, points, train signalling instruments, bells, or gongs.

Points not to be moved without Signalman's permission. (*b*) No person must move any points which lead to a running line, or from one running line to another, without the permission of the Signalman.

Rule 71 forbade Train Register Boys (and others equally unauthorised) from working the signals and points, or answering the block instruments – BR Rule Book 1950, reprinted 1962, BR 87109, p. 78.

Loco Class A3 heading south in 1939, passing Nottingham Victoria Station's North signal box, where Geoff was TR Boy. Photo by kind permission of Rail Stephenson Archive, Charing, Kent.

11. ACCIDENT-PRONE DRIVER T

I recall one incident which occurred whilst I was a TR Boy at the North box. A passenger locomotive B1 type, which we often called a Cloud on Wheels because of the steam which obscured its front when travelling, had been placed on the turntable at the North end for turning by the Driver.

Turntables were required so that locomotives could run engine first, cab rear. They could run the other way round but this was very uncomfortable for the Crew. Heavy wagon sheets or tarpaulins would be put over the end of the tender and the loco cab. When travelling cab first, the footplate could be awash in heavy rain.

This Driver – I will just refer to him as T – a tall, thin fellow, then commenced to push the locomotive from the North end, his Fireman from the South end. It should be appreciated that if one required to turn a steam locomotive, it had to be exactly positioned to enable the table to be moved.

On this occasion, however, T hadn't got it quite right and, after making several attempts to push the locomotive without success, picked up an iron bar with which he endeavoured to lever it round, inserting the iron bar underneath the rails at the end of the turntable. Again he had no success and knew that he would have to get into the cab to reset the locomotive. He threw the iron bar down with great force, on to his foot, breaking his big toe.

He then began to shout his head off in pain. Sammy, seeing what had happened, noticed that T was dancing on one foot and shouted to the Fireman, who was still trying to push at the South end and was unaware of the affair: "Your mate's having a baby."

At this time the Fireman gave up trying to push and went to see what really was the matter. T was taken to hospital, where medical attention was given to him for the broken toe.

It so happened that three weeks earlier T had conducted, ie overseen, a train to Ruddington, South of Nottingham, and, on alighting, had been accosted by a lady passenger who asked him to help her out of the station. The story goes that T assured the lady that he was the right chap to ask, especially as it was foggy.

He took hold of her hand and, taking three steps forward, they both walked off the platform and landed on the track ballast, with T severely spraining his foot. The incident with the turntable was the first day back at work.

I also recall one foggy night when the Signalman at the South end of the station pulled the appropriate lever, causing the semaphore signal to show 'off' for the locomotive to leave the turntable road, ie the rails leading to the table (colour light signals would clear to a yellow or green aspect, depending on the state of the section ahead).

No movement was made by the Driver; because of the density of the fog he could not see the signal. The Signalman therefore telephoned the Shunters' hut and asked one of the Shunters, whose duties were to couple and uncouple wagons, locomotives and coaches from stationary trains, to go to the Driver and tell him to bring his locomotive off the table.

Another 20 minutes then elapsed, with no movement, a long time but, in the horrific conditions, time was the one thing that could be used with certainty of action. So the Signalman asked a Supervisor to go to see the Driver. But there was still no movement.

The Signalman and another Supervisor went together, finding that the first man, the Shunter, had fallen into the deep pit beneath the turntable, breaking his foot, whereupon the second man, the Supervisor, had fallen on top of the first man and had broken his arm.

Both men could not get out of the pit on their own, it was some four to five feet deep, and had to be helped out. The Driver in his locomotive was unaware of the men in distress; fog drowns shouts and cries for help.

The turntable at the north end of Nottingham Victoria Station, where Driver T tried – and failed – to turn his engine round. The deep pit beneath the turntable is clearly visible, to the left of the low safety railings. The photo, by T G Hepburn in 1927, is of locomotive Class B16 No. 2376. The designation S3 on the buffer beam shows its earlier history as (pre-1923 grouping) North Eastern Railways' Class S3. Photo by kind permission of Rail Stephenson Archive, Charing, Kent.

12. FIELD KITCHEN FOR THE TROOPS

Whilst I was working at Nottingham Victoria Station as Messenger and Train Register Boy, Troop trains ran daily, as did Red Cross trains, ammunition trains and later Prisoner of War trains.

Sometimes there were one or two Troop trains a day, on occasion five or six. Some of them transported armoured vehicles such as light tanks and personnel carriers and one could see the Soldiers manning the guns. These trains might be long, with 30 or 40 compartments, depending on the number of Army vehicles.

Red Cross trains carried war casualties and stretcher cases and looked more like parcel trains: because of the stretchers, parcel or newspaper vans were used. Their number varied, according to the situation in France etc.

Ammunition trains were a collection of covered wagons, some short wheelbase, others larger. Sometimes two or three a day ran, sometimes more.

I remember Italians were the first Prisoners of War I saw; there were one or two PoW trains daily. The return of the British Expeditionary Force from Dunkirk I also remember: trains of Soldiers arrived at Nottingham, all dishevelled and without arms, ie their guns and equipment, very little clothing.

The only things they had in their possession were cigarettes, which were offered to anyone for sale at what were bargain prices. One hundred cigarettes for 1s 6d – in today's money about 8p. Scattered amongst the Soldiers were foreign Troops, Poles, Czechs, French, Dutch and Belgian.

As the Royal Army Ordnance Corps was associated with the Ordnance Factory at Chilwell, near Nottingham, these Troops were to regroup in Nottingham and were billeted out on the unsuspecting residents, often without notice, and it could be for months, until the men were posted to other areas for training.

The morale of these Troops was remarkable in that, although they had been given what could be described as a thorough going-over by the enemy, most wanted to go back with better weapons and give the Germans the same treatment that they had received.

To accommodate the Troops, war casualties and Prisoners of War, British Army Soldiers positioned a field kitchen at the North end of the station. This comprised two big tanks, black in colour, with a chimney for the smoke to escape. Soup and tea were the main food and drink offered.

The locomotives of their trains invariably took water at the water column at the North end, near the turntable; there was another water column at the South end.

Steam locomotive boilers had to be filled with water and, to enable this to be done, water columns were positioned at stations and depots. The locomotive Fireman had to climb up on to the top of the tender, dragging with him the chain which was attached to the long, hollow bag of a water column and direct the bag into the tank in the tender. The moveable part of the water column was the water crane.

The Driver would then operate the wheel attached to the column, causing the water to flow through the bag, in effect an extension of the column, and about four to five feet long and 18 inches wide.

On one occasion the Fireman was standing on the tender of a Troop train, guiding the bag of the column into the tender's open hatch, when he accidentally let go of the bag. This resulted in it swinging away from the locomotive, with all the water falling on to the unsuspecting Driver, who stood at the foot of the column. His language was awful and he threatened to do great mischief to the Fireman when he got down from the tender.

Whether he did I don't know, as soon afterwards the signal was cleared for the train to go forward and it did so.

It should be noted that as well as keeping the boiler full of water to enable steam pressure to be constant, the Fireman's duties included putting coal into the firebox to keep the fire up to make steam, taking the coal from its place on top of the tender (the water tank was beneath the coal); working the sandboxes to enable the locomotive to grip the rails when starting from stations etc; keeping a lookout for signals.

On another occasion the Lampman, whose job it was to clean and trim signal lamps in large Signalling areas, was up the 20-foot gantry on No. 4 platform, leaning over the semaphore signal arm, when the signal was cleared for a train. The Lampman was left clinging to the arm as the train passed underneath, thick black smoke being emitted from the locomotive funnel.

The Lampman was covered in soot and suffered from shock, but was otherwise unhurt.

Text from no. 10, responsibility for the cleaning of signal glasses, from British Railways' Instructions Respecting the Cleaning, Trimming and Lighting of Oil Lamps, *BR 29611, 1955, p. 8.*

(i) **Oil lighted signals . . .**

Lampmen are responsible for the cleaning of the glass work (including spectacles) of all oil lighted signals, including the cleaning of the glasses, lenses and screens of the following: –

Banner Signals	Route Indicators
Calling-on Signals	Limit of Shunt Indicators
Warning Signals	Illuminated Permanent
Shunt Ahead Signals	Speed Indicators

. . .

(ii) **Gas lighted signals.**

Same as oil lighted signals – see item (i).

13. CALL-UP PAPERS – AGAIN AND AGAIN

During the time I was a TR Boy at the North box I received my call-up papers from the Government, instructing me to go for a medical examination at London Road Low Level Station. This I did and, fancying the Royal Air Force, applied to join as a Wireless Operator; I had started to learn Morse code.

However, something must have gone wrong, as I had to pass an Army Medical Board (there were different Medical Boards for each Service). They examined every part of me and I was given an A rating; after that there was an intelligence test. I then had to see the Flight Lieutenant, who told me that I would be called up in eight weeks.

I went home and continued to go to work as usual. A fortnight later I received a letter from His Majesty's Government, saying that I had to go again to London Road Low Level Station, for an interview with the Army Authorities.

I therefore presented myself as requested, again being told to go with other male persons to the examination room, where I was to take the intelligence test.

As I had already done this test on the previous occasion, I protested vigorously, to no avail. So I took the test again and, following this, saw a very large person, a mountain of a man, in a private office.

I was not told his name. He was in civilian clothes and told me I had done very well in the test, with 48 right out of 50. He added that I could not be in the front line but would be in the Transportation Corps Royal Engineers, ie the Railway Corps of the British Army.

He did not know when I would be called up but, no doubt, this would be soon. I then returned home to await events. Exactly a fortnight later I again received a letter marked 'On HM Service', which told me to again report to the Army Authorities at London Road Low Level Station.

Again I was told by a man in civilian clothes that I had been kicked out of the Air Force and would be in the Army. I then told this person that I had already been told this on the second occasion I had attended for interview.

Despite this, this stupid person told me that I should have to take the intelligence test again, so I told him in no uncertain terms that I would not do this. He then tried forcibly to push me towards the door of the exam room.

However, I resisted so much he had to give in. "I'll fetch the Sergeant-Major," he said: this he did, the Sergeant-Major being in an adjoining office.

Almost immediately the Sergeant-Major appeared, in full military glory, red sash, and cane under his arm. He halted in his best Guard's manner, clicking his heels as he did so. "What's this I hear, Mr Raynor? All conscripts have to take the intelligence test. Why do you object?"

I quickly told him that I had done this test twice before and that I had no intention of doing it again. As I was at that moment not a member of His Majesty's Forces, he could not make me do the test.

He looked me up and down and then told me to follow him; this I did and went into the office whence he had come, where he pointed to one of the many pigeonholes on the wall.

He put his hand into one and brought out an envelope with my name on in blue ink, which was also marked RAF. This was crossed out in red ink and marked ARMY in big red letters. "Look, the envelope is empty," he said. "All your details have gone to the War Office. You had better wait and see the Officer, he may want to see you."

Following this I joined about 200 other poor wretches in a long corridor with very few seats. I managed to get a seat as I walked further down the corridor than the others, finding that I was sitting opposite an open door of a room containing a desk and two chairs.

No such animal as an Officer was in sight and, as I waited, more men appeared, until the corridor was absolutely full. After waiting about two hours a tall, young Officer appeared, placed his hat on the desk, threw his gloves into his hat and placed his cane on the desk.

He looked into a file that was on his desk and roared: "Raynor!" I immediately walked into the room and closed the door.

"What the hell are you doing here?" were the actual words he said. "I don't know," I replied, "but before I leave here, though, you'll tell me whether I am in the Army, Navy or the Air Force."

"F--- o--!" he said. "And don't come here again." I then left the room and never heard anything further until 1945 when, whilst on duty at Mansfield Colliery signal box, the Station Master's Secretary rang me and asked if I was in a reserved occupation.

I replied: "As far as I know, no." I did not know whether the Railway Company had made me reserved, so I was not in a position to say that I was. I had nothing in writing, no-one had ever said anything.

"We'll have to see about this," she said. But I never heard any more about this again. It should be noted that I did not pass out as a Signalman, which was indeed a reserved occupation, until some time after the episode with the Officer had taken place.

14. RAINWORTH HOPE IN A SEA OF MISERY

My brother, Bill, had been sent to Singapore and in February 1942 my sister got married on the Saturday, the 14th, to Enoch, then a Flight Sergeant in the RAF. Singapore fell to the Japanese on the Sunday, the 15th.

We trusted that Bill was safe and, at the worst, was a Prisoner of War. But we did not get confirmation, official or otherwise, for about another two years, when we received a postcard from him.

It was a blank piece of ordinary postcard with Japanese marks on it. The writing was in Bill's own hand. He said he was all right and a Prisoner of War. "Give my love to Cecily," he said; she was his girlfriend. Later we discovered that he had been dead for six months before we got the card.

On the Monday following the fall of Singapore my mother and father moved into a house at Ransom Sanatorium, Rainworth, near Mansfield. As previously stated, my father went to stay at the sanatorium for six months in 1937.

During that Summer he had been asked to attend a meeting at the sanatorium of the Superintendent, Dr Firth, and County Council* representatives. At this meeting my father was told that he would never again be able to work as he had been doing.

*The 1911 National Insurance Act made local authorities responsible for tuberculosis treatment in their area. The sanatorium opened officially in 1902, prime mover in its establishment being Dr William Bramwell Ransom. Notts County Council took it over in 1914. – *The History of Ransom Hall*, researcher Jean Crooks, editor Vivienne Carmichael, North Nottinghamshire Health Authority, 1998.

The Council would offer him the chance of working only a few hours per day as the Head Painter and Decorator of the sanatorium. The job was to consist of estimating work to be undertaken and supervising about four other members of the Sherwood Village Settlement.

This was a new scheme whereby, following treatment for TB, patients would be given jobs on short hours commensurate with their health capabilities.

Apart from painting and decorating, there were joinery and such-like occupations of light labour. Training was given and the articles that had been made in the workrooms were sold to the public, thereby helping to make the scheme viable.

My father was among the first to be given this opportunity. He was a first-class workman who had served his apprenticeship before going into the Army in the First World War and was recognised throughout Nottinghamshire as a first-rate foreman.

He went into lodgings at Rainworth, working only a few hours a day and he came home at weekends. Then a hostel was provided for the single men and six family houses were built in the grounds for the married men.

The houses were large, very roomy, and very cold in Winter, the emphasis being on fresh air as part of the treatment. My mother had to wear a top coat to get meals in the kitchen, which had no fireplace. She and my father took occupancy at No. 1 Ransom Road on 16th February, 1942.

This scheme was brought about by the Nottinghamshire County Council* and I personally wish to extend to all who participated in

*'Notts. is the only county to have introduced this very necessary corollary to the hospital treatment.' – *Nottingham Journal*, 21 September 1945.

bringing this scheme into being my thanks for giving hope to the sick in what was a sea of misery.

I went into lodgings with my aunt (my mother's sister) and uncle at Mapperley. They were very good to me and I shall always be grateful to them for their kindness during the months I stayed with them.

Bill in uniform, 1941.

15. SIGNALMAN AT SKEGBY

About a month after going into lodgings, I passed out to be a Signalman, ie I passed an examination on Rules, Regulations and Appendix Instructions, which I had studied in my own time at home and work.

This put me on the active service list and entitled me to apply for particular vacancies. Vacancies came up now and again. There were never a lot at any one time, especially if one was selective, wanting something not far from home.

I applied for the position of Signalman at Skegby, near Sutton-in-Ashfield; this was actually a Porter-Signalman's position and, as the title suggests, combined Portering duties as well as Signalling duties.

I was appointed and took up the job in June 1942. Strictly, one had to be 20 to be a Signalman, but the powers-that-be bent the rules so that I could take the Skegby job.

Skegby itself was only a small, rural place; the signal box was at the side of the track. At night the bleat of sheep, together with the hooting of owls, made the place seem weird. With only the light of a hand lamp (containing a vessel with a wick in it) and a Tilley Railway lamp, both giving off paraffin fumes, the signal box took on a life of its own.

I would add that the box was worked on a two-shift system, both Porter-Signalmen ensuring that the fire grate, oven and hob, where we could cook meals and make hot drinks, were blackleaded and polished to such an extent that one could nearly see one's face in

(b) **Boxes where Block Switches are provided—Closing**

The **Closing** signal (7-5-5) must not be sent to the signal box on each side unless one of the following conditions applies:—

   (i) There are no trains in section on each side and the block indicators are in their normal positions.

  (ii) The section between "B" and "C" is clear and there is only one train between "A" and "B", the **Is line clear** signal for which has been acknowledged by "C" by repetition (see illustration below).

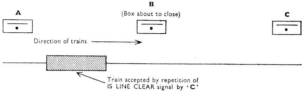

The **Train entering section** signal which has been received at "B" from "A" must, although the train has not arrived, be sent to, and acknowledged by "C".

The Signalman at "B" must, after turning his switch, place the block indicators to the normal position.

 (iii) The section between "A" and "B" is clear and the block indicator for this section is in its normal position, although there are one or more trains in the section between "B" and "C" (see illustration below).

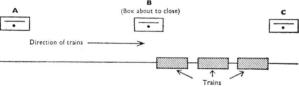

In this case "B" must, after switching out, advise "A" the number of trains that are in the section between "B" and "C", and "A" will again receive the **Train out of section** signal for each of these trains.

When the **Closing** signal has been acknowledged, the Signalman at "B" must then switch out of circuit and clear the fixed signals applicable to trains passing his signal box on the lines to which the block instruments, which have just been switched out of circuit, apply.

The **Testing** signal (16 consecutively) must be exchanged between "A" and "C" when "B" has switched out, and when this has been done, the Signalmen at "A" and "C" must inform the Signalman at "B" on the telephone that all is in order. The Signalman at "B" must not leave duty until he has been so informed.

During the time "B" is closed, the Signalman at "A" must stop and advise the Drivers of trains which are to be cautioned into the section that the caution applies as far as "C".

Closing a signal box, from British Railways' 1972 Regulations for Train Signalling and Signalmen's General Instructions. 'A', 'B' and 'C' represent three consecutive signal boxes, 'B' being the box which required to close.

them. At least once a week the handles of the 20 to 25 levers also had to be polished with metal polish and one could see one's face in them.

Saturdays were a normal working day but Sundays the box would remain closed unless the Divisional Civil Engineer's or the Signal and Telecommunications' Departments were to carry out repair work etc. Signal and Telecommunications personnel were responsible for ensuring that points, signals, telephones were properly maintained, oiled and serviced. A Signalman was then rostered to cover the opening and closing of the box.

The hours of work for both Porter-Signalmen were as follows: the day man took duty at 8 am, swept out the Station Master's office and dusted his desk, and then swept the booking office and front porch. Following this, the day man went to the signal box and opened it as per normal Signalling routine.

Then the box would remain open until the time that a train known to all railwaymen on that Great Northern branch line as the GC* had been signalled, bringing empty coal wagons from Annesley, a Great Central depot, to be detached into the sidings. The locomotive and brake van of this train then left for the Shirebrook/Langwith Locomotive Depot, just inside Derbyshire.

The brake van was the last vehicle of a goods train and on loose-coupled trains the Guard could operate the handbrake (a wheel in most brake vans) to halt the train. At other times he would use the brake when necessary, ie when running down a hill or to hold the train when standing on a gradient. The handbrake on a fitted brake van would not have to be applied. Fitted trains meant that air or

*Great Central and Great Northern were two of seven railway companies that went to make up the London and North Eastern Railway when more than 100 companies were grouped into four on 1 January 1923 (see Appendix for GC Chairman Sam Fay's last message to his staff).

53

LAMPMEN, SIGNALMEN AND OTHERS RESPON-
SIBLE FOR THE CLEANING, TRIMMING AND
LIGHTING OF SIGNAL LAMPS (INCLUDING GATE
LAMPS) MUST SEE THAT THESE IMPORTANT
DUTIES ARE PROPERLY CARRIED OUT.

The term " lamproom " includes all premises used for the servicing of signal lamps.

1. CLEANING AND TRIMMING.

(a) Both the inside and outside of lamps must be well cleaned. Dry cloth or waste must be used for cleaning the lamps and pumice powder, etc., must not be used for brightening. Clean cloth or waste should be used for cleaning the glass work. Methylated spirits, etc., should also be used where authorised.

(b) Men appointed to carry the lamps to and from the signals must keep clean the coloured glasses of the spectacles, also the glass (inside and outside) of the outer lamp cases, and wipe off any loose soot there may be on the expander or pyrometer, where provided. (These are delicate instruments and care must be taken not to damage them or upset their adjustment.)

(c) The chimneys must be kept free from soot and the lenses polished. Ventilation holes must be kept clean and free and no packing placed under the lids.

Left: cleaning signal lamps, in British Railways' Instructions Respecting the Cleaning, Trimming and Lighting of Oil Lamps, 1955, p. 1.

Right: packages, as well as the bulkier goods that Geoff dealt with, were subject to strict rules of conveyance – no. 139 and part of no. 140 in British Railways' Rule Book 1950, reprinted 1962, p. 148.

Rules 139-140

139. Guards and other employees are forbidden to accept for conveyance on any train any description of package, either for themselves, their friends, or the public, unless such package is waybilled, invoiced, stamped, carried under contract, provided with official O.C.S. label, or accompanied by a passenger. Guards must compare the packages with the waybills where used, and note on the latter any defect or discrepancy. All waybills must be initialled or stamped by the Guards.

In the event of any such package being in a damaged condition, the Guard must make a note to that effect on his journal or in his train book.

140. Guards must give careful attention to luggage, parcels, despatches, and other packages entrusted to them, which they must sort in readiness for unloading. Luggage, parcels, etc., which have to be put out must be given by the Guard to the person appointed to receive them, but if the latter is necessarily otherwise engaged, the Guard should place the articles in a safe position, and must call the attention of the station staff to them.

Packages not to be conveyed unless booked.

Guards to compare packages with waybills.

Care of luggage, parcels, &c.

54

vacuum brakes were fitted throughout and when the locomotive brake was applied, the brakes on all the vehicles, as well as the engine, were applied.

Skegby remained open until the GC locomotive and brake van had cleared the section of line between it and the next signal box. Once the 'Train out of section' signal was rung through, the Skegby box could close.

The day man then took up lamping duties. In the Lamp Room adjacent to the signal box he had to clean the signal lamps. These hung on the signal post in a niche behind the red and green shades of the signal, and were covered to protect them from the weather. They were large, glass-sided lamps, about nine inches high and seven inches wide, containing a paraffin vessel complete with wick. He filled them with paraffin and lit them; they lasted eight days.

He then walked to the signals and climbed the steep ladder of the signal post with one lamp or possibly two lamps in his hand, depending on whether the signal was bracketed, ie had more than one signal on the post. Each signal was applicable to a different line, for example Slow line, Main line.

How high he would have to climb depended on where the signal was placed. It could be only about 12 feet; in places to give the Driver a clearer view, it could be 30 to 40 feet. Lamping duties took three days to carry out, Mondays, Tuesdays and Wednesdays, about three to four hours each day depending on the weather.

The day man then returned to the signal box and opened it. He remained there until the afternoon man came on duty at about 12.30 pm to relieve him and allow him to have an hour's meal break, which he took in the signal box.

Following this the day man again took over the signal box and the afternoon man turned to Porter's duties, which took various forms, including assisting Farmers to empty or load rail wagons. The Farmer would have his own men helping but we would see that the wagons were properly loaded to Railway Standards, the sacks and so forth stored safely.

We would count the hundredweight (50.80 kg) corn bags which a Farmer had returned, having hired the bags for a halfpenny a day, I think it was; each bag had to be specially folded. Nineteen bags were placed into one bag, so the 20 bags were ready for the next hirer. If the Farmer was sending produce out in these bags, he had to obtain the bags back. Everything was accountable to him.

The bags then had to be carried to the booking office, where they would be entered up in the day book by the Station Master who, by the way, was the only clerk on duty. He had a Company house adjacent to the station, which had at one time been a passenger train station but in 1942 was not; the Up and Down platforms were still in situ.

One particular job I hated was moving large bags of sheep's wool; these weighed a ton as one had to move them on one's own and you may well imagine the trouble it was to get them along the platforms and down the stairs into the booking office or a wagon. The bags were very dirty and greasy, as well as being hard to grip.

One was greased up to the eyes dealing with them and it took a great deal of time trying to scrub oneself clean on each occasion. We had a supply of hard soap at the station; it was not very good but we did our best.

As well as corn and wool, Farmers loaded sugar beet, potatoes and other vegetables. These went to various towns throughout Britain. There was no cattle dock at Skegby, so we did not load or unload live animals.

After the Portering had finished at about 4 o'clock, the afternoon man relieved the day man, who then left duty; the afternoon man continued as Signalman until completion of work, which could be at any time.

A train of empty wagons was due to leave Colwick, near Nottingham, for Skegby at 10 o'clock each morning and, as it was war time, locomotives were at a premium. Collieries were given low priority against the demand for passenger or Troop trains, ammunition trains, Red Cross trains, etc.

Skegby, which serviced Teversal and Silverhill Collieries about two to three miles away, was somewhere at the bottom of the list and it was therefore about 10 o'clock at night before the train arrived to commence work.

The Colwick train took its 60 empty wagons to Silverhill Colliery and returned with a full load of 50 to 55 coal wagons which it detached in the sidings at Skegby; it picked up the 60 empty wagons that the GC had left that morning and took those to Teversal, again bringing a full load of 50 to 55 coal wagons back.

The train then went forward to Colwick Sidings where the wagons, all for differing destinations, could be sorted. Skegby signal box had to remain open until the train had cleared the section ahead.

On this line the sections became longer or shorter depending on what signal boxes were open or closed. Pleasley was the box between Skegby and Shirebrook and, if closed, it took 20 minutes for a train to run from Shirebrook to Skegby, uphill all the way.

It was more often than not 4 o'clock in the morning when the Signalman finished work. As I was at this time living with my mother and father at Rainworth, I had to cycle 16 miles back home; this meant that I had to cycle a total of 32 miles a day to and from work. In addition, I was still a member of the Home Guard. When I went to live with my mother and father, I had to join the Home Guard at

Mansfield. They did not do night duty as we had at Nottingham but there was a muster of personnel on Sunday mornings, when we attended drills, and we trained on the moors one night a week.

I was also courting Janet, who was then living with her parents at what is known locally as the top of Carlton Hill, and at times I was absolutely fagged out. But I still kept going.

Janet in Land Army uniform, 1942.

16. LUCKY TO GET HOME AT ALL

During the 18 months or so that I was at Skegby I experienced the worst travelling conditions that I have ever known. This was one Friday/Saturday night in the Winter of 1942-43 when for once I finished work at about 12.30 am.

There was a slight drizzle which turned to ice as soon as it fell, causing me to slide all over the place. When I attempted to get on my bike at the top of the station slope I fell off and, despite two further attempts, finally had to start walking home, dragging my bike behind me.

I had to cling to every available fence, hedge or post and at road junctions I had to get on my hands and knees, still dragging my bike behind me. Indeed, when crossing the Sutton/Mansfield road, I had to do this, hoping no cars or lorries would appear.

Fortunately I got across safely and, when I did reach home around 6 o'clock, my rubber cape was completely covered with an inch of ice. I was lucky to have arrived home at all.

One other thing I did at Skegby was to be passed out by the District Signalling Inspector on the Single Needle, a Railway form of Morse code; this form of communication was to enable Railway messages to be passed from station to station, signal box to signal box, or vice versa.

A special instrument was worked by moving a handle left or right: left was dot in Morse, right was dash. The Single Needle instrument could be used over a wider area than the telephone. Each box, station or office equipped with this instrument had their own call

Regulations for train signalling on double lines by the absolute block system—*continued*

17. STOP AND EXAMINE TRAIN (7 consecutively)

(a) Signalmen must be careful to notice each train as it passes to ascertain whether there is any apparent necessity for having it stopped at the next signal box for examination.

If a Signalman observes or becomes aware of anything unusual in a train during its passage, such as signals of alarm, goods falling off, a vehicle on fire, a hot axle-box, or other mishap (except a tail lamp missing, a tail light out, or a train divided, for which see Regulations 19 and 20), he must, after the **Train entering section** signal has been acknowledged, send to the Signalman in advance the **Stop and examine train** signal. He must also exhibit his signals to prevent any train from proceeding on the line used in the opposite direction except when he is satisfied that such line is not affected; if, after a train on the opposite line has been stopped, the Signalman has reason to believe that such line is not affected, the train may be allowed to proceed after the Driver has been advised of the circumstances. The Signalman in advance must also be advised of the reason for sending the **Stop and examine train** signal.

(d) Should the **Stop and examine train** signal have been sent on account of a door being open on a passenger train the Signalman sending the signal must advise the Signalman in rear, and trains running on the same or opposite line between these signal boxes need not be detained to await evidence that the line is not obstructed but the first train in each direction must be stopped, the Driver informed of the circumstances and instructed to proceed cautiously to the next signal box, keeping a good look out. If, however, the section is short and the Signalmen can satisfy themselves by observation that it is clear, it will not be necessary for trains to be cautioned.

Rule 17 which (a) said that Signalmen must take note of each train passing and (d) referred to the 'Stop and examine train' signal if a door was open – British Railways' Regulations for Train Signalling and Signalmen's General Instructions, 1972, p. 25.

60

sign: Skegby's was KB. The longest message I ever took on the Single Needle was whilst I was a Signalman at Sutton-in-Ashfield, about a year later, in respect of the movement of goods parcels etc.

The message was actually to the effect that no goods parcels except Naval, Army or RAF stores were to be allowed to go to the following places: this was followed by every port and coastal village or hamlet, town or city from the Wash right round to, and up, the Bristol Channel, a prelude to D Day, the Allies' invasion of Europe.

Prior to this, the Eighth Army, which had been successful in Africa against Rommel, came home; most of them were sent by rail from the ports to regroup for the invasion.

I well remember the Troop trains bringing these Soldiers, each train being stopped numerous times en route as the doors were open; passenger stock was used to convey the Troops and some carriages had doors at each compartment, others had doors at each end of a carriage.

In the vestibules, where two coaches were coupled together and passengers could walk through or reach the toilets, men were seated on the floor with their legs outside.

Of course this was quite contrary to the Railway's Rules and Regulations. No doubt the lads were glad to get back and didn't give a damn for the Railway Rules. But in the positions they had taken up, any one of them could have fallen from the train, causing death or injury.

The trains were stopped by Signalmen to prevent this happening. Signal boxes had been placed either side of the line so that Signalmen could observe the handles and doors as trains passed.

One Signalman, seeing the open doors, would send the 'Stop and examine train' Block Bell signal to the next signal box. The

Signalman receiving this signal, seven beats on the Bell, would place his signals against the oncoming train.

It was strange that some of these Desert Rats, as the victorious Troops were called, subsequently appeared on the moors behind the house where my mother and father lived at Rainworth. They had tanks and light track vehicles and were firing at various targets and carrying out manoeuvres with the infantry.

I was very interested to see them when I was off duty. The American Army then began manoeuvres on the moors in a similar fashion to the Desert Rats.

I well remember the day of the invasion of Europe and listened avidly to all the news reports and the progress of our Troops. It was truly an historic time and all the people were of one mind to get the war over.

The doodle bugs, the German flying bombs which dropped silently from the sky, had by this time caused a lot of sudden death and destruction and the people of Britain had had to suffer this without much hope of combating it.

By May 1945 the German Army was defeated, total surrender being made, but the Japanese war continued in the Far East, with the 14th Army becoming more successful in Burma and the Americans winning naval battles in the Pacific.

VE Day was celebrated by the populace and there was great rejoicing, with the Government expressing their determination to finish off the Japanese war.

Finally the Japanese war was ended, following the dropping of the two atom bombs on the mainland of Japan early in August 1945, and I well remember cursing Clem Attlee, the Prime Minister, for declaring VJ Day* at midnight.

I was booked to work 6 am to 2 pm at Rufford Junction signal box so, the evening before, I waited until 11 o'clock before going to bed, but there was no announcement on the radio then. I therefore did not hear that the next day would be a holiday.

I arrived at Rufford at 5.55 am, only to be told I need not have bothered to go to work. To my mind it was a typical Labour way of doing things.

My family and myself waited for news of Bill, my brother, learning of the terrible conditions that the British Prisoners of War had experienced at the hands of the Japanese.

We prayed that Bill had survived, however. Although confirmation had been received from the War Office that Bill was a Prisoner of War and we had had the postcard from him in his own writing, we still didn't hear anything further.

Some time after VJ Day a fellow Soldier, who had been in Bill's Company of the Signal Corps, arrived home in Nottingham, where my sister, Gertrude, and her husband, Enoch, lived. He had been a Prisoner of War and was reported as saying that Bill had died in

*Japan's surrender on 14 August 1945 was announced simultaneously in Britain, the US, Russia and China. The following two days, 15 and 16 August, were celebratory holidays.

Burma. My brother-in-law heard this from his Barber and made efforts to see this man, who agreed to come to Rainworth to tell my parents what he knew. No word from the War Office had been received.

The Soldier told us that Bill had been transferred from his unit when they arrived at Singapore, Singapore Fortress as it was described, and sent by the Army Authorities to Fortress Signals, a Regular Army Battalion, not conscripts, as Bill was.

He had seen Bill in Changi Hospital after the British had surrendered and learned that Bill was working as an Electrician in the hospital whilst being a Prisoner of War. It appeared that later Bill had gone up country, into the Malaysian jungle, with Indian Troops.

We were told by the Soldier, who was at Changi Jail throughout the war, that he had read a notice posted up on the wall saying Bill had died in Burma, but he could give no further information.

Other members of Bill's unit were contacted when they came home and, from what they said, it appears that the Japanese had told the British Army Authorities that they were to build a new Railway in Burma.

It would be better all round for the British Prisoners to go to build the Railway, they said, as the food was better and the conditions would be beneficial for them.

In view of this the British Army Authorities sent, with the first batch of Prisoners to go, those Soldiers who had been either ill or wounded and were recuperating in the hospital. All these men travelled 1,000 miles in overcrowded Railway cattle trucks in terrible conditions with very little water, no proper sanitation and a number of casualties.

When the train arrived at the rail terminal, it was found the medical supplies had been left behind. The Japanese said that these would be sent up later. THEY NEVER WERE. The Prisoners then marched hundreds more miles before the camps were reached.

Bill had been sent with the second load of Prisoners up country; they had travelled in much the same way as the first. Bill was known to have been in the notorious Nikki camp, along the Burma-Siam Railway near the border with Burma, where there were numerous deaths.

I learned from returning Prisoners that cholera in a Dutch camp in the North had travelled down the river to other camps. Nikki was on this river, which provided the Prisoners' drinking water, with consequent results. In fact most of the camps situated on the river had suffered. No medical supplies were given to combat the disease and therefore there were many deaths.

Out of the first batch of 1,000 Prisoners sent to build the Railway only three returned; two were so ill they were walking skeletons, the other was completely mad.

Enquiries were made to the Authorities but nothing came of this. Then, six months after the war with Japan had finished, the War Office finally told us it appeared that Bill had died either of cholera or dysentry, they could give us nothing definite.

We did have notice from the Authorities that Bill had been identified as being a carrier of cholera, tests being made whilst he was in Nikki camp by Army Medical Staff who were also Prisoners. He was on his way to a hospital when he died. One of the Prisoners said later that he had buried Bill, and he said Bill had died of dysentry and exhaustion.

All this was a tragic loss to us, as can well be imagined; none of us will ever get over this, the scar is always there. What a waste of a life which had such promise.

65

To think that a person like Bill, who was such a clever chap and was thought to have a bright future in front of him, should have his life thrown away by incompetent Generals and Government.

I ask myself even today, as I look at the generations who followed the Second World War, what good had it done for men like Bill to give up their lives in this way?

My thought is that whoever creates war, or encourages others to take up arms, should be the first to be sent to the front, regardless or who or what they are.

Bill's resting place, block B1, row O, grave 10, in Thanbyuzayat War Cemetery, Burma.

In the September of 1946 Janet and I were married; she was at the time working at Messrs Richard Lunt's Warehouse for clothing, soft furnishings, etc. Because of the difficulty in getting a house we lived with a widow in her bungalow some 200 yards from my mother and father's house.

There had been little or no housebuilding during the war and a points system was being used for housing. Janet, who had been four years in the Land Army, was given a rating which meant a three-year wait for a house. I, being a civilian, ie not in the Services, was given a nil rating.

However, it was a very nice bungalow and we enjoyed living there. We lived along with Mrs Revett although, of course, we had a bedroom on our own, and we paid 10/- a week. Mrs Revett used to leave us on our own for a fortnight or month at a time whilst she visited her relatives in Leicester.

After about eight months we had to find alternative lodgings when, at the age of 68, she went to Australia to get married again – her new husband, earlier in life, had been the boy next door! It was the second marriage for both of them and, following a month's honeymoon in Australia, they went to live in New Zealand.

Just before Christmas 1946, I had forgotten to chop some sticks for lighting the living-room fire the next day and, in consequence, took a torch into the nearby garden hut, which was used as a store, and commenced to do this.

Unfortunately, whilst in the course of bringing the hatchet down on to the wood I was chopping, the torch – which I had placed in what I thought to be a safe place – fell and I brought the hatchet down on my left thumb, nearly taking the top off.

The local taxi owner took Janet and I to the nearest hospital, ie Ransom Sanatorium, the chest hospital my father attended.

The doctor in charge was not available and, as there was not a casualty department, the Deputy Superintendent, Dr Galloway, a lovely lady Doctor who looked after my father, together with another female Doctor, and the Matron with two staff Nurses and another Nurse, commenced to stitch the top of my thumb back on.

It should be noted that the Matron was a very respected figure in a hospital. She was totally in charge of the Nurses, Cleaners, Porters, etc. WE COULD DO WITH THESE MATRONS NOW!

They all seemed to enjoy the operation except me, who could not let my species down; I was not given any injection or painkiller. Dr Galloway did the stitching, my arms and legs being held forcibly whilst the needle was pushed through the nail.

Dr Galloway said it was a nice change to do accident work again and it had brought back a load of memories. Following this, I personally was in a state of shock; it was therefore great to be given a strong cup of sweet tea and I slowly recovered.

They did a good job as the thumb completely healed, without showing a scar. I expressed my appreciation to all of them and always had a soft spot for Dr Galloway, who was at that time getting on in life.

She even healed a big spot on my chin which my Doctor, although giving me various remedies, could not do. She prescribed Gentian Violet and this liquid, when brushed on, did the trick almost immediately.

I was off work for two weeks with the cut thumb and, as there was no sick pay provision at that time, had no money coming in.

Janet in 1944, two years before she and Geoff were married.

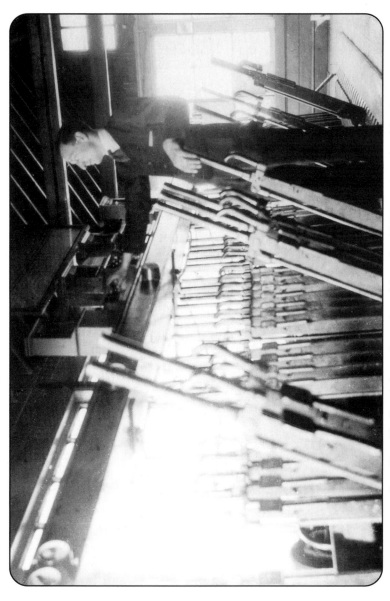

Geoff at Rufford Junction signal box in 1955, using the block instruments on the block shelf above the signal levers.

On arriving back at work, the terrible winter of 1947 began. At first only two or three inches of snow lay on the ground and I was able to travel over the moors on my bicycle, as was my wont, the three and a half miles or so to Rufford Junction signal box where I was Signalman.

However, it became no joke when the snow kept coming and drifts on the moors were higher than a man. I well remember having to turn back towards home one day with the snow up to my waist, the bike having to be held up in the air over my head as I walked back to civilisation. From then on I had to get to the box by other means.

This necessitated having to walk to Mansfield Station, some three to four miles away from home, and then to travel on the Mansfield Concentration Sidings pilot locomotive from Mansfield Station to Rufford Junction.

Mansfield Concentration Sidings was a marshalling yard some five miles from Mansfield Station where trains, mostly of coal traffic, were formed. The pilot locomotive helped in shunting movements or forming trains, and normally was used only at this depot.

Along with me from Mansfield Station were the Signalmen of four other signal boxes, and Yard Staff – Shunters, Lampmen, Greasers (the men who put grease in the axleboxes of wagons), Carriage and Wagon personnel. All this, nine or 11 men, when the number of authorised persons allowed to ride on the footplate of a locomotive, beside the Driver and Fireman, was two.

Of course, this was classed as an emergency and the powers-that-be turned a blind eye to it, although the arrangement went on for weeks as the roads were blocked.

On the road from Mansfield to Rainworth buses and cars, as well as lorries, were buried under the snow, there being only a path about two feet wide running the whole length of the road.

I did manage on one occasion to go by bus from Mansfield to Clipstone Colliery, which lay some three-quarters of a mile from Rufford Junction; the signal box at Rufford controlled the lines to Clipstone.

On getting off the bus, I had to travel down the Colliery branch line to the signal box by clinging to the top six inches that remained visible of the wooden boundary fence between Colliery land and private fields; I would have been lost in the snowdrifts if I hadn't done so.

I relieved my mate at 12.45 pm and he then told me that he was going to knock off sick. I had to stay on duty until relieved at 8 o'clock the following morning.

The conditions were atrocious and no trains could get through; snowploughs were sent along the sections but there was always a problem when snowploughs were used.

Platelayers, or Snowmen as we called them, were on duty to clear the points and the rodding which connected the signals to the levers in the signal box; these men worked valiantly to clear the snow, only for it all to be pushed back by the snowplough. It took hours to clear the snow from these points etc and one often wondered if it was worth it.

At Kirby-in-Ashfield, some 25 miles from Mansfield Station, on the GC main line from Sheffield to London – the Kirkby signal box also controlled the Mansfield Branch line – a passenger train was blocked in the cutting, the Driver describing the snow as being up to the locomotive funnel. Until assistance could be given, the Driver and Fireman brewed tea from the locomotive boiler for the passengers and themselves.

It was some hours later that help came, Platelayers and Army Troops having to dig a patch through the snow to the train before the passengers and Crew could be released.

The train stood there three weeks before it could be liberated. When this was done it was found that a gas tank on the rear of the train was derailed; the breakdown train had to attend to do the rerailing, all the time with the likelihood of an explosion.

Passenger trains which ran locally, eg Nottingham to Derby, Nottingham to Lincoln, were authorised to carry a gas tank as the last vehicle, for the gas to be offloaded at various depots. Outlying areas did not have gas supplied by any other method. Heigh-ho! primitive times!

Signalmen's General Instructions—*continued*
Working during fog or falling snow—*continued*

Where special instructions are issued to a Signalman permitting him to call out the Fogsignalmen (outside their normal working hours) before the fog marking point is obscured or visibility is reduced to a distance of 200 yards, Absolute Block Regulation 4(e) should not operate until the fog marking point is obscured or he cannot see for a distance of 200 yards, as the case may be.

When snow falls to such an extent that signal lights are liable to become obscured or the lights or spectacles become covered or partially covered by snow adhering to them, arrangements must be made for the lamps and spectacles to be cleared of snow. After sunset, until the signals have been attended to, the provisions of Absolute Block Regulation 4(e) must be applied.

The prescribed course of action during falling snow, or fog – British Railways' Regulations for Train Signalling and Signalmen's General Instructions, 1972, p. 151.

The long, cold winter of 1947 lasted from January until the end of March and was followed by a lovely, hot Summer.

In the early part of June I joined the Relief Staff, a promotion which meant that I covered a number of signal boxes. If a regular Signalman was off sick or on leave, I covered his shift. This meant having to travel to far away signal boxes linked to a home station or base.

My home station at first was Mansfield Station. Later, to cut down the travelling time and thereby cut costs, this was changed to Shirebrook (a station, as well as a Locomotive Depot with Langwith), then Edwinstowe and then Mansfield Concentration Sidings.

A Relief Signalman was paid, in addition to his own Grade rate, travelling expenses calculated on the basis of 20 minutes to the mile or, if it was cheaper, a lodging allowance of something like 30 shillings. Therefore, when my home station was Mansfield and I worked at Mansfield Colliery signal box, three miles away, I was paid 60 minutes' worth, ie an extra hour in my wage packet.

This helped to raise one's standard of living, but had its drawbacks. These were that Regular Signalmen did not often have day-shift days off.

Most Regular Signalmen preferred to work the night shift for the enhancement pay of the night rate; one can easily see that the Relief Signalman would be working afternoons, or forced to work 12-hour shifts, afternoons and nights being the times the Regular

Signalmen took off to go out with their families. Some Signalmen would only take their holidays when on the afternoon shift. There were also vacancies to cover, as as well as sickness.

Examples of the bell signal codes used between signal boxes – British Railways' Regulations for Train Signalling and Signalmen's General Instructions, 1972, p. 6.

Regulations for train signalling on double lines by the absolute block system—*continued*

Bell Signals—*continued*

See Regula-tion	Description	Code
6 and 12	Train out of section, or Obstruction Removed	2–1
7	Blocking back inside home signal	2–4
	Blocking back outside home signal	3–3
	Train or vehicles at a stand	3–3–4
10	Locomotive assisting in rear of train	2–2
	Locomotive with one or two brake vans assisting in rear of train	2–3–1
11	Locomotive arrived	2–1–3
	Train drawn back clear of section	3–2–3
12	Obstruction Danger	6 consecutively
16	Train an unusually long time in section	6–2
17 and 20	Stop and examine train	7 consecutively
19	Train passed without tail lamp	9 consecutively to box in advance; 4–5 to box in rear
20	Train divided	5–5
21	Shunt train for following train to pass	1–5–5
22	Train or vehicles running away in wrong direction	2–5–5
23	Train or vehicles running away in right direction	4–5–5
24	Opening of signal box	5–5–5
	Closing of signal box	7–5–5
	Closing of signal box where section signal is locked by the block	5–5–7
26	Testing block indicators and bells	16 consecutively

75

21. BIKE ACCIDENT AT CLIPSTONE 'RAT HOLE'

As a young boy I was always frightened of the dark and remained so until reaching adult age. What I was frightened of I could not at that time describe; it was later that I found it was really myself that I was afraid of, that I had to look my fears in the face and conquer them with the help of God.

On the way home from the afternoon shift when the moon was high in the heavens, pedalling my bike with 10 or 15 miles to go, I felt my spirits rise and it was at these times that I felt the presence of God. At other times, when it was raining, snowing, frosty or foggy, my spirits would be very low and I had some dreadful journeys.

Due to the many miles I had to travel on my pushbike, I bought a new BSA Bantam motorbike, which really did make travelling much better. At first my wife, Janet, would not ride pillion, but eventually she gave way and really enjoyed the experience.

In November 1951 I had the misfortune to come off my motorcycle and become concussed at a place known locally as the 'Rat Hole' at Clipstone. There was a series of bends, mostly very sharp, and my bike skidded on black ice as I was on my way to relieve the Signalman at Clipstone East Junction.

The time of the accident was approximately 5.45 am and in my groggy state I knew that there was a Miners' bus to Ollerton Colliery some way behind me and that I must get to my motorcycle before it came. I made valiant efforts to get to my bike but found myself unable to walk the short distance. I actually found myself going away from it. I therefore had to crawl on my hands and knees, and eventually reached it.

Alas, I then passed out completely, falling on the motorcycle tank. Luckily the bus Driver saw me and was able to stop his vehicle short of where I lay. I was then picked up by the bus Crew. The bus took me some eight miles further on to Ollerton Colliery Ambulance Room and I was then taken to King's Mill Hospital, three or four miles from the centre of Mansfield, where I was detained.

About three hours later Janet arrived, having been alerted by the Railway Authorities after they rang the Hospital Authorities. She did not know for two hours what had happened to me and therefore both of us ended up in bed, Janet suffering from shock and I from headache and double vision.

I asked for a light job for a few weeks to get back to normality. However, I was given a job which meant that I had to travel on my motorbike about 30 miles – 60 miles there and back – with both feet on the ground, at very low speed, in snow and ice. I never again asked for a light job!

Text from rule 16, which provided a glossary, and an interesting Note (i) about women employees (BR Rule Book), pp. 18-19.

16. Except where otherwise provided, the –	
Term	Includes
Ballast train	Engineers' materials train.
Driver	Motorman.
Electric token	Electric staff, tablet or key token.
Engine	Electric or other locomotive.
Fireman	Assistant Motorman or Second Man.
Freight train	All trains not composed of coaching stock.
Multiple-aspect signal	Signal capable of showing more than two aspects.
Passenger train	Mixed train, i.e. train conveying passengers and goods.
Telephone	Telegraph.
Station	Depot, yard or halt.
...	
Train	Light engine, i.e. engine without a train; also rail car, rail bus.

Notes. – (i) Where women or juniors are employed the Rules and Regulations apply to them as to men.

A relaxing moment for Geoff at Welbeck Colliery Junction signal box in 1957.

22. TERROR AT WELBECK

On at least two occasions I have been frightened to such an extent that all use and power have completely left me.

On both occasions it was when I was relieving at Welbeck Colliery signal box, which was about four miles from where I lived at the time and was situated in a deep cutting with fields either side. The Mansfield Woodhouse to Edwinstowe road passed over a bridge over the Railway some 300 to 400 yards from the signal box.

It was pitch dark. Inside the signal box there was one electric light above the small desk on which the Train Records book was placed and in which the times of trains had to be set down, eg the time the train was offered, and accepted; the time the Signalman sent the 'Train entering section' Bell signal to the box ahead; the time he gave the 'Train out of section' signal to the box in the rear; also the time the signal box ahead gave the 'Train out of section' signal.

There was also, of course, a Railway paraffin hand lamp, which could be used to give a white, green or red light to Drivers and Guards, and a Shunter's pole, or large pole about seven feet in length, with a metal clip at the end which was used for hooking wagons together.

My Relief had asked me to stay later than 10 pm on this day as he wanted to go into Mansfield to see a certain film at the local cinema, so I had agreed to him arriving at 11.30 pm.

At about 9 pm, when things were quiet, no trains about, there was a loud sound of laughter, as made by a mad person, at the Edwinstowe end of the road bridge. The laughter continued at intervals, travelling across the bridge and down the field at the back of the box. Sheep and owl noises I was used to, but this was terrible.

I locked the windows and door, and waited to see what would happen. The sound of feet on the steps of the signal box was then heard but, as I peered through a window, I could not see anything.

Then a face appeared, pressed to the window directly opposite me. I realised that the person was Sunny Chilvers, my Relief, who was supposed to be at the cinema.

All kinds of feelings swept over me and he laughed his head off as I collapsed into a chair. His explanation was that he had decided not to go to the cinema, having missed the hourly bus from where he lived.

The horrible laugh he had made was that of a hyena of India, where he had been stationed during his Army career.

If I had had the strength to hit him I would have done so but, alas, I just didn't have any and it took me all my time to leave the signal box and find my bike to go home.

The second time I was so terrified was when two men escaped from Rampton, the Hospital six miles South of Retford for people who have committed crimes but are judged to be insane. They spent two days in the house of the Signal and Telecommunications Engineer, who was based at Tuxford, having hit the Engineer with an iron bar and assaulted the wife.

After they left the couple managed to contact the Police, who then made wide searches for the two men. They had escaped on the Thursday and were still at large on the Saturday night.

When darkness fell, the knowledge that these desperate men

remained free did nothing to bolster my spirits. I had to wait for a train of empty wagons to arrive from Lincoln and it was to stop at Tuxford, which was only 10 to 15 miles East of Edwinstowe, and, of course, the men might well travel on this train.

About 9.45 pm I heard the noise of footsteps crunching on the ballast of the line near my signal box. This ballast was of ash, the residue of coal burned in locomotive fireboxes, in Steel Works' furnaces, etc.

Again, fastening the door and windows and holding the shunting pole in my hand, I awaited the inevitable. Feet were then heard on the box steps and I tried my hardest to see who was coming.

A face appeared at a window next to the door, a truncheon beside it. "I've looked into those sheds and I can't see anyone," said the Policeman.

There were, about 100 yards from my box, three tool and meal sheds belonging to the Signal and Telecommunications Staff and the Civil Engineer's Staff.

I let the Policeman into the signal box and again all the tension and strength went out of me. The Policeman was only young but he was brave – I would not have gone into any of those sheds to look, not if Old Nick was behind me.

23. IN CONTROL AT DONCASTER

By 1957 I had obtained exam results of 85-86% in Signalling and Operating Studies, which I had done in my own time in a Correspondence Course run by British Railways Management, and which culminated in the examination.

I had reached the top as far as the Mansfield Area was concerned, a division which covered parts of Lincolnshire and Derbyshire as well as Nottinghamshire, from Sutton-in-Ashfield to Mansfield, to Clipstone, Ollerton, Langwith, Cresswell.

However, by then I no longer wanted to stay in the Signalling service. My main aim was to be in a higher earning position to provide more satisfactorily for Janet and John.

Another reason that I went from Outside Staff to Supervisory Staff, such as Assistant Controller, was that there was a better pension scheme in the Staff and Salaried grades. Over the years this proved to be the case.

I therefore began to look around for other jobs. Among these were jobs for Controllers, for which Signalling was basic training, and I had two interviews, one for Rotherham and one for Doncaster, before I did actually get an Assistant Controller's job at Doncaster. At the interview one had to show one was fully knowledgeable of the Operating side of the Railways, of the geography and topography of the Railways in your own and other Signalling and Operating areas. Being a Relief Signalman expanded one's knowledge, also studying for the exam which I had passed.

This meant leaving Mansfield Woodhouse and taking up lodgings at

Doncaster until I could get a house there. This I did, lodging with a retired British Transport Policeman and his wife.

Janet had not wanted to go to Doncaster and hated the thought of leaving Mansfield Woodhouse, where we had moved into our first house in April 1949 after living in rooms owned by other people. The house had three bedrooms and was mortgaged, of course, but we were on our own.

In the end she gave way with reluctance and only later in life, when retired, thought that it had been good in terms of our pensions.

Therefore on the day that our only child, John, was two years of age, 13th July, 1958, we took residence in a newly built three-bedroom house (mortgaged again) at Scawsby, North Doncaster. It had a medium-size garden and, eventually, a garage.

Working in the Control Office was very different to working on the Outside Staff. To give the reader some idea of what a Control Office did during the period of 24 hours, seven days a week, 52 weeks a year would take up a considerable amount of time and would probably be boring; however, I will give a brief account.

Doncaster Control Office observed part of the East Coast Main line and all the lines into and out of Doncaster Station on the North side. Control was open continuously in 1958, but in the mid-1960s it was closed at 6 o'clock on Christmas morning so that Christmas Day would be a holiday for all Railway Staff, and it reopened on Boxing Day morning.

The Head of the Control Office was the Chief Controller and he was only in the office during what was known as Office Hours, 08.00 to 17.00 hours.

The other members of the Staff were on duty at differing times, as each Circuit had to be manned continuously. Each Circuit Controller

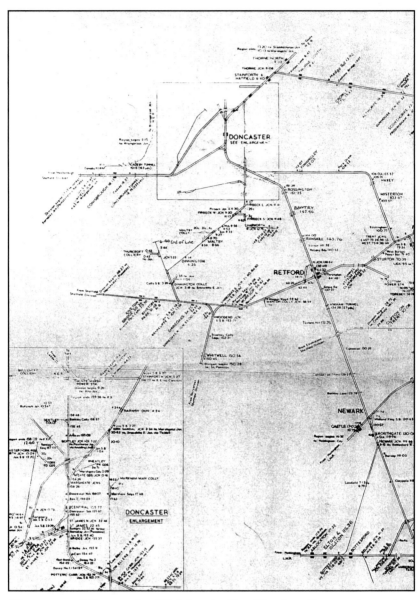

The area of Doncaster Division in Geoff's day: the western side (above) and the eastern side (facing page). BR map.

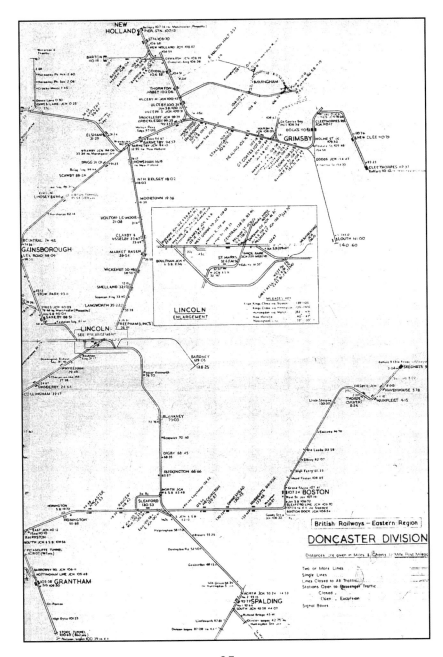

British Railways – Eastern Region

DONCASTER DIVISION

85

sat at a desk, his headset attached to a console of 40 to 50 telephone lines. He was connected to an open circuit which covered all the area he supervised, signal boxes, stations, yards, level crossings, etc.

He could ring out to each and talk to all when necessary. During the war he would pass over to all in his area the message Yellow! which meant an air raid was in operation as enemy planes were crossing the coast. Red! meant that they were about to be overhead.

Communication could be made with other Circuit Controllers, Police and Emergency Services, as well as private individuals, eg to obtain the services of the Civil Engineer's Staff, home if necessary; if hours had been extended without prior notice, advise the wife!

One could get anywhere through the telephone console. BR had a very extensive telephone system. When later I joined the Signalling and Accident Section I could get through to practically any station, yard or office on British Rail. Each had their own call number. I spoke to Liverpool Street Office, Waterloo, Scotland, Wales without any trouble whatever. Just ring the right number – clarity was brilliant!

The route mileage the Circuit Controller was responsible for was of differing lengths, some being of many miles. To enable him to have complete supervision over an area, its topography – signals, signal boxes, yards, etc – would have to be considered as a whole.

For example, No. 6 Circuit took control from the South face of Stoke Tunnel at Hydike, South of Grantham on the East Coast Main line (100 miles from King's Cross, London, and the start of Doncaster Area) to Loversall Carr, about four miles South of Doncaster Station (more than 150 miles from King's Cross).

It should be noted that these distances were so measured because all tunnels, stations, yards, etc, on British Rail had a location mileage, shown on posts erected on the side of the line. No 6 Circuit also controlled the line from Loversall Carr to Gainsborough Trent Junction in Lincolnshire over the Joint Line (which was originally jointly owned by the Great Central and Great Northern Railways).

Everyone was trained on another Circuit, as well as having his regular post, to enable them to relieve that other Circuit in extreme circumstances, ie sickness etc. In addition Relief Circuit Controllers worked up to seven different Circuits, so they were very valuable people; their knowledge was very extensive.

Three weeks' training was given on all jobs within the Control Office. You were expected to become competent within that period and to remember how to do any job, even if those three weeks were all the practice you had.

Circuit Controllers' desks were placed facing the walls of the room. Behind them were other Controllers, eg Train Crew Relief Controllers who, as their name suggests, arranged for trains to be crewed up, Locomotive Controllers who allocated locomotives to trains. At the end of the 1960s Maintenance Controllers were appointed to ensure the diesel fleet was properly maintained and taken out of service for examinations.

At the beginning of a shift the Train Crew Relief Controllers and Locomotive Controllers would have at their desks lists of men and locomotives available for passenger and goods trains, but due to late running, derailments and other eventualities, they would have to amend their lists. Once they had the information, they passed it to the Circuit Controller.

As far as the Locomotive Controller was concerned, he took a locomotive off the trains as soon as it became available; it was a hand-to-mouth situation. The shortage of engines was apparent throughout my Railway career, both before and after the Beeching cuts.

87

Part of a diagram (below and facing page) showing new colour light signalling at the south end of Doncaster station - from LNER (Southern Area) circular RR 451.

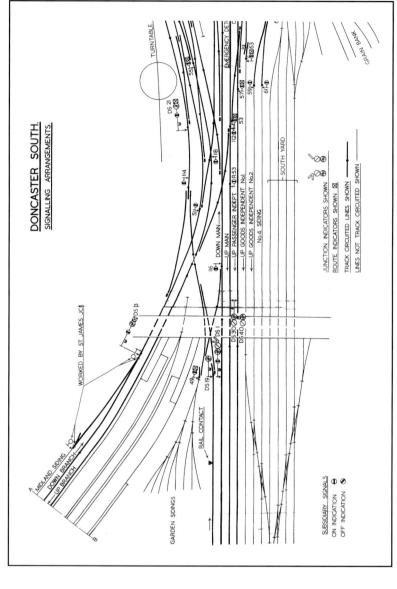

DONCASTER SOUTH.
SIGNALLING ARRANGEMENTS.

JUNCTION INDICATORS SHOWN ⊠
ROUTE INDICATORS SHOWN ⊠
TRACK CIRCUITED LINES SHOWN
LINES NOT TRACK CIRCUITED SHOWN

SUBSIDIARY SIGNALS
ON INDICATION
OFF INDICATION

88

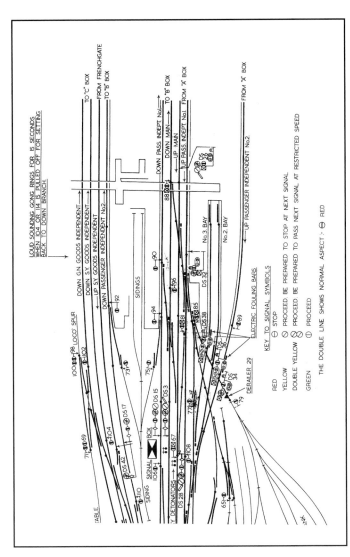

Notice of the changeover to colour light signalling at Doncaster South was given on 8 September 1947. By the time of the second and final stage – new signalling at Doncaster North, announced on 31 August 1948 – the Railway Executive, British Railways, Eastern Region, was in charge. The 1948 circular, RR 455, referred to the signalling recently introduced at Doncaster South.

The Assistant Controllers, of whom I was one, wired information to other Controls on the loading of trains and the details of Crews: Driver, Fireman and Guard.

Each Control position was given a classification, Class 1, Class 2, Class 3, Class 4, which showed the level of responsibility for each job undertaken. I joined as Assistant Controller Class 4. Class 1 was the highest position, next to the Deputy Chief Controller.

The loading of trains differed considerably. For example, King's Cross Control would ring me on the telephone console and give me the train number, loco, Crew and time on duty, followed by details of the destinations of the vans on the train.

If this train detached vehicles (vans) in the Doncaster area, the Yard Foreman would give a fresh loading of the train, with details of new vehicles which it had attached. This fresh loading would have to be given over the telephone to the Controller at York, the next Control point, by the Assistant Controller when the train left the yard. Departure times were given as well.

At 09.30 hours every morning except Sunday, a member of the Management Team joined other Management Teams of Controls at King's Cross, York, Leeds, Darlington, Newcastle and Regional Control (our HQ) to discuss the troubles and trials that had been experienced throughout 24 hours.

They also worked out the provision of wagons in the Freight Fleet to the various firms which had ordered certain vehicles, eg steel wagons and bulk-carrying type of vehicles.

On Sunday a similar meeting was carried out by the Deputy Chief Controller on duty with his opposite numbers as above.

24. CARD-CARRYING TRAINS

The Deputy Chief Controller was in charge of the office during the period of one shift, ie 06.00 to 14.00 hours, 14.00 to 22.00 hours and 22.00 to 06.00 hours. He had an Assistant, one of the Assistant Controllers, whose job was to analyse the running of trains throughout the Doncaster Area.

In short, contrary to public thought, all express trains, ie all passenger trains and 75% of freight trains, were subject to running analysis; some had penalties for late arrival. Coal trains and slow trains which ran at 35 mph were not analysed at that time.

A train 'card' or prepared form was made out by Passenger and Freight Office Staff, giving details of each train in the working time-table.

Excursion or freight special trains had their own card made out in the Control Office, as these trains were agreed with Regional Control during the shift. On this card were printed the names of the signal boxes, stations, yards, etc, which the train had to pass on its journey throughout the Doncaster Area.

If a train lost *one* minute, this had to be accounted for in the overall analysis. Imagine a poor fellow coming on duty at 22.00 hours to act as the Deputy's Assistant throughout the night – he had to estimate from the train cards the actual running of all the trains until relieved at 06.00 hours.

This would not have been so bad if all trains ran in their correct order and kept time; however, some trains such as fruit trains (in season) were hours late and the delays had to be notified to other

Controls and Regional Control; parcel trains during the pre-Christmas period were also hours late. Signal failures, locomotive failures, level crossing incidents, weather conditions, derailments – a thousand and one things all had a bearing on the running of trains.

This was a time when, during the night hours, the East Coast Main line was run more or less at line capacity, ie no more trains could be accommodated, with the inevitable result that when a train failed there was a knock-on effect of heavy delays.

Additional to the working time-table, cattle trains conveyed animals from agricultural areas and West coast ports serving Ireland to Smithfield in London or abattoirs en route; fish trains from Hull, Grimsby and Aberdeen ran daily to various destinations all over Britain; rhubarb trains ran from Wakefield, where fields of it were grown, to Covent Garden in London.

Circus trains, mostly seasonal, saw all the animals and tents, etc, loaded into special vans, and it was always an occasion when the animals were detrained at any town. The elephants always led the circus company through the streets, lined by crowds or following to where the circus was to be held.

Stage props were conveyed by special trains composed of special vans when a West End play was moving to the provinces, or vice versa.

A British Railways Inspector was in attendance at all loadings to see that they were carried out in accordance with the British Railways Loading Manual. It should be noted that British Railways were unable to refuse any consignment as they were 'Common Carriers'. I believe this was later cancelled, but I don't know when.

To book a consignment, the Clerk had to consult a book which covered the whole range of commodities that one could possibly think of, all in alphabetical order: the weight of the goods concerned, the type of vehicle needed to move the goods, all this before a price could be given.

The poor Deputy's Assistant, by the time 03.00 hours came, was at a low ebb and, although there was an agreement to have a 20-minute break each eight-hour shift, he had no time to do so. In fact, whilst I was at Doncaster, from April 1958 to January 1961 and again from 1967 to 1969, I never did get a food break, even when working 12 hours on a stretch, to cover holidays, sickness or vacancies.

The only thing the Management did towards helping the Staff was to allow a Controller on 12 hours to get a meal from the British Railways Canteen at lunchtimes, but this was only whilst the Control Office was at Hexthorpe.

In 1959, I think it was, the whole of Doncaster Divisional Manager's Organisation, including Control, left the Hexthorpe offices and went into newly built Gresley House, adjacent to Doncaster Station. This was named after the great Sir Nigel Gresley, LNER Chief Mechanical Engineer who designed, for example, Pacific steam locomotives, such as the speed record-setting *Mallard* and *The Flying Scotsman*. The Pacifics, specially made for passenger expresses, were built at Doncaster Plant Works.

All food and drink at Gresley House was taken at your desk on the second floor, as you were plugged into the telephone circuit, both giving and receiving instructions as to the running of trains.

Paying particular attention to showmen's and similar vans – part of rule 158 (d), BR Rule Book, p. 166.

Furniture vans, showmen's vans and similar road vehicles, on their own wheels, empty or loaded, must have the wheels scotched and fastened to the trucks by ropes, straps or chains, and, in addition, the leading end of the van bodies must be secured to each side of the railway trucks by ropes passed over the cross-bar (generally known as the body bolster bar) underneath the van bodies, the ropes being afterwards tightly braced.

93

25. CREWS WOKEN BY 'CALLER-UP'

Derailments, suicides or motorists colliding with BR property, such as gates or barriers, all had to be dealt with by the Deputy Chief Controller and his Staff. The Emergency Services had to be alerted, also any BR Staff such as Linemen, Technicians, Civil Engineer's Staff, when their special skills were required.

The Signal and Telecommunications Engineer, or Lineman as we referred to him, needed to ensure that the mechanism of gates or barriers was able to be operated; lights could be damaged. Linemen were responsible for the electrical side of the Railways: maintenance of signals, telephones, points, etc, as well as gates and movement of gates.

The Civil Engineer's Staff needed to ensure that the track, ie sleepers, rails and ballast, was not damaged and that posts etc were all right or should be replaced. These Staff also looked after fencing and crossing gates.

Should a derailment, fall of rocks in a cutting or any such incident occur whereby trains could not travel over the section of line, arrangements had to be made for buses to cover Railway services. The Deputy Chief Controller on duty would have to contact bus companies. As these companies have few reserves, this was always a problem.

Several companies had to be contacted to provide the service required. The Deputy then had to advise the Police Authority through whose area the bus or buses were to run of the service being given, the service it was covering and, also, the Commissioner of Police at Leeds had to be informed every time.

Freight trains affected were either cancelled or diverted, where this was possible. In addition, diversions had to be organised and this would inevitably result in train Crews having to be changed or conducted, ie overseen by someone who knew the route, if a given Crew on any train did not have the required knowledge.

Should this be so, then the Train Crew Relief Controller would have to alter the rostered Crews' orders and manipulate the Crews accordingly.

One such Controller, Fred, was a very experienced man and, when he told the Circuit Controller that 'Pete Wissey' was the man appointed to work a train, the Circuit Controller knew at once that Fred hadn't a clue but was working on it – there was no such person as Pete Wissey. It always caused merriment among the Staff.

In 1958 Doncaster had a certain number of men, Drivers and Firemen, for scheduled services; one Driver was additional to requirement to every five men, although this was often reduced by sickness, leave, etc. The same applied to Guards, but they were usually more flexible.

Guards did not have to be trained on diesel locomotives like Drivers and were not at one time or another at Training Schools. They were available to work trains for which they had route knowledge once they had mastered working the brake valve and handbrakes, light switches, couplings and pipes necessary to ensure the safety of the train, also the brake chains, mostly over doors.

It should be appreciated that if a member of the train Crew was rostered 'spare', he could be moved two hours either way; for example, if he were due to commence duty at 10.00 hours, he could be brought forward to 08.00 hours or put back to 12.00 hours.

Train Crews were at this time woken up during the night hours by a 'Caller-up', who was specially employed to go to the Driver, Fireman or Guard's house and knock him up about an hour before he was due on duty. The 'Knocker-up' would not leave a house until the person he required was actually at a window or the door to acknowledge the call.

The 'Knocker-up' would also tell the spare Crew member of his changed duty, giving him at least an hour's notice. Where possible, he would be informed earlier.

The Railway Authorities were therefore very particular as to where the member of the train Crew lived. Anyone living outside the call-up area was severely frowned upon and had to make his own arrangements to get to work on time.

In addition to the above, Crews on long-distance trains had to go into lodging after their turn of duty was completed. Drivers and Guards had to have 12 hours' rest between duties.

An example of this would be that a King's Cross Crew working a train to Newcastle or indeed Edinburgh would be relieved on the disposal of the train, ie placing it in sidings or a station platform bay, and then go into a Railway Lodging Hostel, which was specially provided for such Crews.

These hostels were only provided at specific places. One was at Birmingham, where Crews from Frodingham – the locomotive depot at Scunthorpe was known as Frodingham – went into lodge after working a train carrying steel from Steel Works at Scunthorpe. They would be rostered to work a train of steel from Scunthorpe to Birmingham, then go into the hostel and, following this, work a train of empty steel wagons back to Scunthorpe.

Another hostel was at Ilford and was still operating until the 1960s, I believe, when lodging in hostels was stopped. Faster trains and a different way of running trains was used. Relief Crews en route made lodging unnecessary.

The 12 hours' rest between duties did not apply to other Staff. Outside Staff such as Shunters, or Signalmen, could be called back in nine hours. After a weekend shift, the Outside Staff could be called back in eight hours.

Relief Controllers were not exempt! I have left Rotherham Control Office, where I was working from 1961-65, at 14.00 hours, arriving home at about 15.00 hours, only to find a telegram already there, calling me back at 22.00 hours for 12 hours' duty.

A 1964 amendment to rule 127 (iii), requiring a driver unfamiliar with a route to be conducted over it and spelling out the duties of a Conductor (rule 127 (iii), BR Rule Book 1950, reprinted 1962, pp. 128-129).

RULE 127. Clause (iii)—Amend to read :—

(iii) If not thoroughly acquainted with any portion of the line over which he is to work obtain the services of a competent Conductor.

The Conductor must give to the train Driver the necessary instructions in regard to the signals, curves, gradients, speed restrictions, and other characteristics applicable to the line over which they are working and leave the actual driving entirely in the hands of the train Driver.

The Conductor will be responsible for the due observance of signals, speed restrictions, etc., and safe working of the train.

In every case the train Driver must study the signals, speed restrictions, and other characteristics of that part of the line over which he is being conducted.

The Conductor will be responsible in cases where it is necessary for the Fireman to carry out the provisions of Rule 55, for seeing that this is done. In the case of trains or engines, the driving cabs of which are single manned, the Conductor will be responsible for carrying out the duties laid down for the Fireman in respect of Rule 55.

2.5.64

97

TRAINMEN

EGER	Provide conductor between points named for driver of _____
ALERT	Provide conductor between points named for guard of _____ to _____
FRANK	Provide guard to work undermentioned train. Ack.
CEDAR	Instruct driver and guard of undermentioned train, as follows.
SLOE	Instruct driver and guards of undermentioned train to stop instead of slipping vehicles.
BOYNE	There will be no water at the following station.
CLYDE	There is now a supply of water at the following station. Instruct drivers.

(See also DUTY)

TRAIN WORKING

COWARD	May I attach the following to undermentioned train?
CLOTH	Be prepared to detach undermentioned leaving here next to locomotive on following train.
CLIMB	Be prepared to detach undermentioned in middle of following train.
COW	Be prepared to detach undermentioned leaving here in the rear of the following train.
TURBOT	Be prepared to deal with following on undermentioned train.
ARPASS	Reply by wire stating number of passengers, or percentage loading in the following train/s leaving your station _____
SLIPPER	Vehicles can now be slipped as booked.
SKUNK	Secure connection with _____
ARNO	Undermentioned notice received.
BAY	Passengers in undermentioned train for _____
BARN	No passengers in undermentioned train for _____
HAGUE	Do you agree to train named stopping at _____?

Train Working (Continued)

CHARIOT	Following train will stop at _____ to take up or set down undermentioned party. Advise all concerned and see that no avoidable delay occurs.
LINEAR	Ordinary working now resumed.
STONE	Traffic being worked on single line.
HANOVER	The following train will be divided as under. Advise all concerned.
PRUNE	The following train requires assistance in rear from _____ to _____
URE	It is important for following reason that undermentioned trains should be worked punctually. Do all that is necessary, so far as you are concerned.
WEDGE	The following, vehicle (or vehicles) to work through.
SLOG	Wire arrival time destination.
PINE	Cancel the running of trains as under.
SLOE	Instruct driver and guards of undermentioned train to stop instead of slipping vehicles.
CALVIN	Following train will run as under. Advise all concerned.
CAPE	Undermentioned train will not run. Advise all concerned.
CICERO	A special train will run as under. Advise all concerned, and note.
ACACIA	Special train as under left (or leaving) at _____
VENLO	Special empty train running as under.
RUPEE	Load the undermentioned train sufficiently light for following.
YANKEE	_____ special train to run as laid down in working time tables with passengers for (or off).
CREOLE	Arrange to work forward.
FOCUS	Arrange to strengthen the undermentioned train or trains as shown.
FORMAY	Wire formation of _____ train, commencing from locomotive.

c

Eger and Alert – telegram codes, from Standard Codes for Telegrams, BR 87222, 1958.

26. EGER AND ALERT YORK

The manipulation of train Crews by Relief Controllers was a very exacting job and when I entered the Control Office at Doncaster the Train Crew Relief Controllers were very experienced.

On commencing duty the Relief Controller would receive from the Timekeeper at the Locomotive Depot, and from the Guards' Timekeeper, a list of men who were to take duty during his shift and the trains they were to work. Shortages were always with us and, of course, it was the Train Crew Relief Controller's job to ensure that all essential services, express passenger trains mainly, were crewed up throughout.

If this was not possible, eg the man appointed had not the whole route knowledge, he would send a telegram or telephone the next Control Office to say that the train was 'Eger' or 'Alert' at some given point, say York.

In the standard code used by BR, 'Eger' meant that the Driver did not know the route beyond York and 'Alert' meant that the Guard did not. The message would be similar to this: Crew of 1A26. Eger and Alert York.

Therefore the Control Office at York had to cover the Driver and Guard from that point. This could be done either by a new Crew or by appointing a man to conduct the Driver or Guard over the route the train was to run.

Another difficulty which arose was that some Drivers were not familiar with the traction, ie the type of locomotive, and had not been trained to work it.

This, of course, became worse when dieselisation was considered the new form of traction and diesel locomotives became more the workhorse of the Railway, as opposed to steam.

It should be appreciated that there is a tremendous cost involved to bring a new type of locomotive into service. Planning, administration, tooling-up, etc, take a lot of money.

New types of diesel locomotives kept coming into service from about 1955, passenger types, freight types, shunter types, gradually delivered by the companies which had contracts to build them, such as English Electric.

This meant more training of Crews became necessary, which also meant that whilst these men were being trained, there were fewer men to work trains, a vicious circle. Imagine the difficulties to cover crewing of trains when diesel locomotives came into use with more sophisticated electric mechanisms.

There was also a shortage of locomotives for the number of trains required. All the time I was at Doncaster, and indeed whilst I worked at Rotherham and Sheffield Control Offices later, this shortage was always with us.

The locomotive fleet was such that each depot had a number of locomotives attached to it. Shortages could be caused by late running, accidents, going into main works for repairs and maintenance. Steam locomotives, when they were the prominent traction, were subject to the same shortages.

Locomotives could also be misused by other regions. When I was at Doncaster Control, we sent a loco to Crewe for a general overhaul. It was missing for about nine months.

Then one of our chaps went down to Southampton and he happened to see it being used by Southern Region. What had happened was that Crewe Control Office sent the locomotive on a job down South and Southern Region just kept using it.

It should be noted that we did the same thing with other regions' locomotives. The Locomotive Controller at Doncaster used Midland engines and he got into trouble for this.

Before, and after, the Second World War excursion trains, as well as scheduled passenger trains in the working time-table, were run to the seaside towns. Also excursions were run for such organisations as the Women's Institutes for their members to travel, say, to Coventry to visit the new Cathedral.

It should therefore be appreciated that depots were always short of the full complement of locomotives to carry out the working time-table. Very often, as soon as a locomotive, steam or diesel, had completed one job, it was immediately used for another.

So much for what Dr Beeching thought, that there were too many locomotives at the time of his Plan in 1963; he ought to have been there juggling with what we had, both before and afterwards.

Anybody could have done what he did, cut and cut. What he failed to do, and what they're still failing to do, is to build, to do things. Demolition is the easiest thing, making things is not.

Every holiday time, eg Christmas, Easter, Spring Bank Holiday, orders would be given for five or six locomotives to be sent from Doncaster to King's Cross to cover the expected Relief Trains required to convey the overspill of passengers for booked trains to the North of England.

However, the locomotives might have a wasted journey. The public were very fickle. On the day when the excursion was due to run, if it happened to be very wet before the train or trains were due to leave, there were few people who would bother to arrive.

Quite a lot of people would not get tickets until half-an-hour or so before the departure time. If only one person arrived at a station where an excursion was to leave, British Rail had to run the train.

British Rail Staff would ask the one passenger whether he or she would like to travel on a service shown in the working time-table. If the passenger agreed, they would cancel the train. If not, the excursion had to run.

The introduction of diesel locomotives gradually expanded until 1968, the year when steam locomotives were withdrawn from regular service.

For six months in 1965 I was acting District Freight Rolling Stock Inspector at Rotherham, necessitating me to walk into Steel Works, Collieries, Chemical Works and Factory premises.

During this time I had occasion to visit Beighton, the main depot of the Civil Engineer, British Rail, where track mounted on Railway wagons was marshalled and other equipment used by his Staff was kept. Certain wagons only used by the Civil Engineer were also stored there. These could contain ballast, eg stone for making the bed for the rails.

The depot was adjacent to Tommy Ward's, a firm which bought and dismantled condemned Railway vehicles such as wagons and passenger rolling stock, where I saw a number of steam locomotives standing in all their majesty.

Over the next few days, still checking on wagons etc at Beighton Depot, I witnessed these magnificent 'beasts' gradually disappear before my eyes.

They seemed to start dismantling them from the top right down, from the cab and boiler, together with the steam chamber and funnel, and it really was a shocking thing to see.

27. FLYING SCOTSMAN

In 1958 the practice was to have a passenger type of locomotive standing in a bay or the sidings at Doncaster Station called the station pilot, with its funnel facing towards the North and its cab rear. Another was at Retford, Nottinghamshire, with its funnel pointing South.

These were to be used to haul trains where steam locomotives lacked steam because a valve had become defective and they lost power, becoming unable to maintain the scheduled speed. This was known as 'priming'.

The normal position of a locomotive is to run funnel first, so the pilot at Doncaster would be used to relieve a train going North and Retford pilot would be used on trains going South.

It should be noted that a passenger type of locomotive would be a Pacific, which had a wheel arrangement of 4-6-2. This meant it had four small wheels at the front, two on each side; the next six wheels (three on each side) were 6 feet 8 inches in diameter, then two smaller wheels (one on either side). The wheels on freight traffic locomotives had smaller diameters.

It should not be taken for granted that passenger locomotives were not sometimes used for freight work, but this was avoided when possible.

Pacific types of steam locomotives were equipped with scoops or large suction bags which were attached to a locomotive tender. By moving a lever on the locomotive the Fireman lowered the scoop into troughs provided at specific points, eg Scrooby between

Retford and Doncaster. These troughs contained piped water and when the scoop was lowered the water, by means of a vacuum created by the locomotive, was drawn into the tender.

The trough was refilled in the same way as a toilet in the domestic house, the water level being controlled by a ball valve, which enabled water to be released into the trough.

It has been known for a Fireman to lower the scoop too early, the scoop thereby being knocked off and lost. Therefore the train had to make an unscheduled stop at a water column some distance up the line, mostly at a station. Yards also had water columns, which were positioned either side of the line.

With the withdrawal of steam locomotives from service, this meant that water columns, water troughs and indeed coaling plants within depots, where tenders were filled with coal, became obsolete and were consequently dismantled. This meant that difficulties could be experienced with such events as the *Flying Scotsman* locomotive 4472 hauling a passenger train.

One such occasion occurred when I was working in the Doncaster Control Office as General Relief Controller, during the second time I took duty there. Alan Pegler, who owned a family firm in Retford, rubber manufacturers called The Northern Rubber Company, had bought the locomotive in 1963.

He had organised with the British Rail Authorities to take a train of steam enthusiasts from Cleethorpes to King's Cross, returning late in the evening.

On this occasion he was not providing coal, water or buffet facilities and most of the afternoon was taken up ensuring that the Fire Brigade was on hand with their machines' sufficiently wide hoses to pump water into 4472's two tenders and that a local coal merchant was in the right place with the required amount of coal and had the

104

proper equipment to place it in the tender. A request was also made for food and provisions to be supplied for about 300 persons.

This, of course, was only one train with a privately owned locomotive and for one such train to take up most of the Deputy Chief Controller's time to my mind was a waste of time and money.

It should be noted, however, that Mr Pegler had a contract with British Rail which meant that when the *Flying Scotsman* was hauling a train, it was deemed in law to be on hire to British Rail. It was in effect a BR locomotive while pulling a train.

On another occasion, also a Saturday, it was learned that 4472 had developed 'priming'. It was standing at Boston, having been employed by Mr Pegler to take steam enthusiasts to London from Cleethorpes and was on its way back somewhere around 22.00 hours.

As I had just come on duty I received the request for a locomotive to be sent to haul 4472 and the rest of the train into Cleethorpes from Boston and thence into Doncaster, where the train was to terminate.

That particular night it was my job to allocate locomotives to trains and I therefore had to contact the nearest depot, Immingham Diesel Locomotive Depot, to supply a locomotive. A Brush Electrical D1501 was the one nominated, being prepared and manned.

This locomotive was prepared and crewed up by Immingham Depot and sent off shed, ie out of the depot area, subsequently arriving at Boston where it was attached to the front of the train, hauling 4472 and the passengers to Cleethorpes, where the Fire Brigade and coal merchant were waiting.

Diesel 1501 had then to reverse locomotive 4472 and the passenger stock, or carriages, so that it could haul them to

Doncaster, arriving there in the early hours of Sunday morning. Just imagine the scene that Summer's morn, about 300 persons of both sexes and all ages and sizes standing on the Dock, the area (leading from the station towards the bus station) immediately in front of Gresley House and behind the No. 1 platform.

Some years before, a cattle dock stood at this location. Cattle were entrained and detrained there, as were circus animals and stage scenery.

All the 300 steam enthusiasts were well behaved, looking towards where the train was standing on the Down Passenger line with diesel locomotive 1501, locomotive 4472 and stock, in that order.

There did not seem to be even a rustle whilst the Shunter uncoupled the stock from the two locomotives. Neither was there any movement until the locomotives had proceeded forward under the North Bridge, over the crossover road, where points were arranged to enable a train to run across from one line to another, and had come to rest to await the Signalman changing the route.

When this had been done, locomotive 1501 proceeded to push 4472 from Down to Up line and, as soon as this started, all the 300 people went mad to get photographs of what would appear to be 4472 hauling 1501. What some people will do truly amazes me.

28. GOOD WORKMATES AT ROTHERHAM

In 1961 I took duty as Assistant Controller Class 3 at Rotherham Control Office, having by then taken another examination following from the British Rail Correspondence Course and gaining 86%.

I put in for the position on the Rotherham Control Relief Staff when it was advertised. One had to take the opportunity when it presented itself. Promotion was limited at Doncaster at this time, although that altered when Lincoln Control was incorporated by Doncaster Control later in the 1960s, when Control Offices were amalgamated by British Rail to cut costs.

There were seven positions I had to cover: No. 1, No. 2, No. 3 Circuit Controllers' positions; Locomotive Assistant Controller; Crew Relief Controller; Passenger Assistant Controller; Deputy Chief Controller's Assistant.

Rotherham Control, incidentally, was the very first Control Office, and it was opened by the LMS Railway Company. It supervised the area of line from Horns Bridge (near Chesterfield) to Cudworth (near Barnsley) via the Tapton-Rotherham Masborough section known as the 'Old Road' (at Tapton the line diverged into the New Road to Manchester via Dore or to Sheffield Midland Station).

It also supervised the route Chesterfield to Sheffield and Barnsley, and Conisbrough to Wath (electric traction) on the Dunford-Guide Bridge-Manchester line.

Although I had to travel by car to Rotherham each day, more than 30 miles there and back, I thoroughly enjoyed working there, and my colleagues and workmates were very good friends and helpers.

In 1965 I was appointed a District Freight Rolling Stock Inspector Rotherham by Sheffield Divisional Manager's Office; Rotherham Control was now under this Divisional Office, the two having been amalgamated.

The Inspector's position was advertised as being temporary, but it actually lasted six months and was to be good experience for future promotion. I applied for it because I wanted to further my knowledge of Railway working.

I also learned a great deal of how outside firms operated using Railway wagons, sheets and ropes. My eyes were opened to what firms will do to cut costs and use whatever comes to hand for their own purposes.

A redundant Passenger Stock Inspector was subsequently made District Freight Rolling Stock Inspector on a permanent basis and I had to revert to the Sheffield Control Office.

As a Rolling Stock Inspector I had a desk in an office in the detached building situated in the apex of the line where the Holmes Curve and the 'Old Road' joined just before reaching Rotherham Masborough Station.

I did not spend much time in the office, which was located in Masborough Locomotive Staff Office. The duties I had to perform were to ensure that the correct records were kept by the firms which used British Rail freight wagons, sheets and ropes.

Among the places I had to visit were Parkgate Iron & Steel Ltd, South Yorkshire Chemicals Co and Rotherham Gas Depot, all in a group of firms between Roundwood and Swinton on the Masborough-Cudworth line.

I also checked on Roundwood Yard itself, a BR yard about three miles from Masborough Station which, although officially closed, was used to stable condemned Railway wagons, ie those with no more useful life, and also wagons that required to be cleared because firms had not completely emptied them of materials.

We actually found one to be a third full of manganese – quite a costly content yet discarded by the firm, whose details had by then been removed from the wagon.

I also had to visit another BR yard, Masborough; Templeborough Steel Works at Sheffield; three Collieries and, in addition, Tinsley Marshalling Yard which had recently opened between Rotherham and Sheffield.

High-ranking members of Foreign Governments came to see Tinsley which was of a revolutionary design and contained main and secondary yard sorting sidings, the length of the roads holding up to 80 standard wagons.

To give the reader an idea of how long this was, the number of wagons that could be conveyed by trains travelling over the East Coast Main line from Doncaster to King's Cross was equal to 52 wagons, or single length units.

The Dowty system of automatic wagon control had been installed to overcome difficulties associated with conventional retarders in hump yards. So, for example, the roads at Tinsley featured booster/retarder units.

Wagons from trains were run into respective roads depending on their destinations. To illustrate this: a train of loaded wagons would run into the reception sidings located on the Eastern side of the complex. The locomotive was detached from the train and took up its next working.

The wagons were inspected by a Yard Shunter located at the reception sidings and he made up a list of 'cuts', uncoupling

Tinsley's eastern approach and the reception sidings. Diagram (on this and facing page) from Tinsley Marshalling Yard, DUP:KX:220/65, British Railways, Eastern Region.

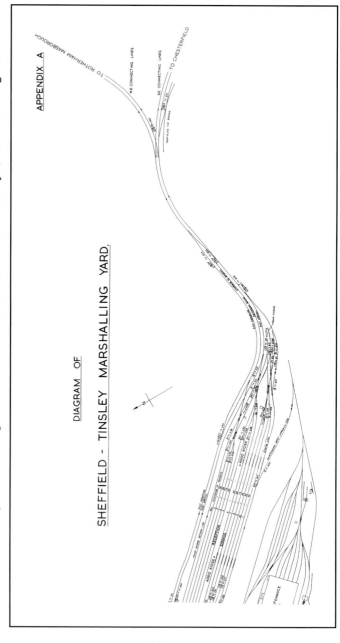

APPENDIX A

DIAGRAM OF

SHEFFIELD - TINSLEY MARSHALLING YARD.

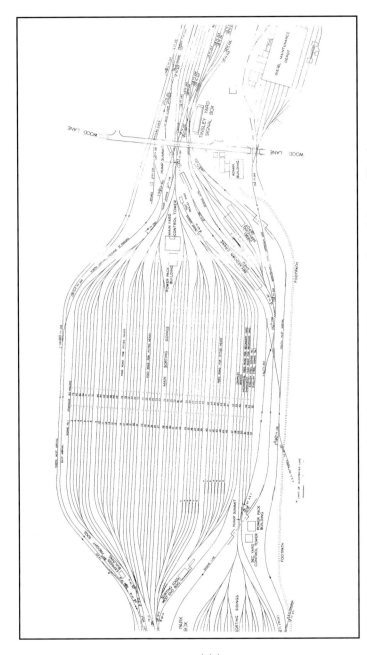

Tinsley's main sidings, west of the reception sidings. Tinsley was the last modern marshalling yard to open, in 1965.

between wagons according to where they were to go. The list was then placed in a transmitting machine within a kiosk. This was linked to a receiving instrument in the Main Control Tower in which the Yard Inspector was located. The information on the list was fed to the point-setting control machine, ready for the Yard Inspector to commence the shunting-out of the train in the reception sidings.

In the meantime a special locomotive, with a 2 mph (3.2 km/h) speed locking device incorporated in the driving controls, was positioned behind the train at a given signal from the Control Tower.

The locomotive then commenced to propel the train forward at not more than 2 mph: this allowed the leading wagon or wagons to travel slowly over the hump, which caused them to increase speed, leaving the rear wagons from which they had been detached.

The point-setting control machine, acting on the Shunter's instructions, operated the points, making the necessary movements to enable all the wagons to run into their respective roads. Wagons for the secondary yard passed over the main yard hump, carried along the mechanical feed road (or, if that could not be used, the emergency feed road) to the secondary yard hump, and then were sorted into the appropriate sidings.

If the wagons ran either too fast after negotiating the hump or too slowly, the booster/retarders positioned on the inside of the rails caused the wagons to increase or reduce their speed as necessary. Of course, some wagons ran more easily than others and did not need the booster/retarders to operate. The booster/retarders were of metal construction; I forget the actual pressure on the oil of the hydraulic system but this must have been high.

My job at Tinsley was to walk through the yard to ensure that sheets, ropes and wagons were properly used, not damaged superficially (the Carriage and Wagon Inspector was responsible for the metalwork, brakes, etc), as per Railway Loading instructions.

Just as I got my bearings as Rolling Stock Inspector, there was a Guards' strike which paralysed the Railway. Trains were stacked all over the place. Tinsley Yard was no exception and most of the roads within the complex were full.

I, with three other Inspectors, was given a Bardic hand lamp, a sheaf of papers and a wooden clipboard, and told to record details of the wagons in each road. This we did and I claim to have walked on every bit of ballast in the yard whilst doing so.

It took several days to record the complete detail on wagon labels, such as destination, vehicle number, etc, and identify the road the wagon was in.

Often I had to read the information by means of the lamp, which was battery operated and usually supplied to Guards, Drivers and Shunters. It could display a white, yellow, green or red light, depending on which shade had been selected to cover the bulb by turning the switch on the head of the lamp.

It could be attached to the rear of a train if the red tail lamp had been broken, the Bardic lamp displaying its red aspect.

Text from the description of Tinsley's secondary sorting sidings – Tinsley Marshalling Yard, p. 5.

Secondary Yard Sorting Sidings

These comprise 25 sidings in 4 balloons and are numbered 60 to 84, each with a capacity of 31 standard wagons.

Traffic for the Secondary Yard is routed direct from the Main Yard via the Dowty hydraulic Mechanical Feed Road.

Westbound departures proceed via the Secondary Yard Westbound Departure Line. The Secondary Yard Shunt Spur is to the south of this line.

Eastbound departures do not normally take place from the Secondary Yard but a route is available via the Secondary Yard Eastbound Departure Line which passes under the Main Hump before joining the East Departure Line.

29. ORDERED OFF TREETON COLLIERY PREMISES

As previously stated, part of my duties was to visit Collieries, necessitating my walking on rough track within the Colliery premises, ensuring that the Colliery Staff were not misusing Railway wagons, sheets and ropes.

When walking within various premises, one often found that Railway sheets were being used for many different purposes. Each sheet had holes drilled through the waterproof fabric and a brass ring was then positioned where the hole had been. A number was displayed identifying the sheet as Railway-owned property.

I found one such sheet under about a ton of sand. A corner of the sheet was just visible, with the brass ring showing. I had the firm remove the sand to release the sheet.

Of course they didn't like doing it but when I reminded them that I knew the sand had been there for over six months, a demurrage fee (of, I think, 1d per day) being owed to British Rail for its property being on the firm's premises, they changed their minds.

Another sheet was found to be used by a lorry Driver. He too was loath to take it off the load his lorry was carrying, but did not like paying demurrage.

Once, at Treeton Colliery, some four miles East of Sheffield, I was asked to leave by the Colliery Manager.

He found out that I had been stationed by British Rail one afternoon at the Weigh Office, loaded end, keeping watch as to the number of wagons being loaded per hour and the number left in the empty sidings at the end of the shift. He ordered me off the premises at about 20.00 hours. This I did straight away.

The reason for the Manager to be so hostile was that each Colliery required a certain number of wagons to commence a shift. Treeton Colliery loaded wagons on a two-shift programme commencing at 06.00 hours and carrying on until 22.00 hours.

It was the practice to order from British Rail 150 wagons to start the day shift and therefore the onus was on BR to get these wagons to the Colliery before 06.00 hours so that the day shift could commence loading.

This, of course, was the daily order; however, should the Colliery not load 150 wagons each day, this left a surplus in the Colliery empty sidings and therefore the figure of 150 wagons required for the next day was not true.

On the day I was given the order to go off the premises, the Colliery had not loaded the wagons that had been placed in the empty sidings and were not likely to do so by the time the afternoon shift finished.

The surplus, plus the 150 wagons ordered, would have given the Colliery a figure exceeding 200 wagons which, to all intents and purposes, meant that shortages could have arisen at other Collieries and firms, and indeed often did.

The wagon fleet was such that, as with locomotives, there were often shortages, partly down to Beeching's cuts again. Most used were coal, steel and special wagons.

Coal was carried in merry-go-round wagons of hopper-type shape and in 'minfits'. It was whilst I was working as District Freight Rolling Stock Inspector that the new kind of coal train came into usage known as merry-go-round trains. These just kept going, eg between

Colliery and Power Station, Power Station and Colliery, in a continual round of fill and empty.

Steel wagons could be several different types and each type had a different name, Bolster was one, plate was another. Special wagons were kept strictly for carrying particular commodities, eg Cartics conveyed cars from works to depots, for example from Dagenham to coast ports, for conveyance eventually to foreign ports.

Weltrol was the type of wagon that could convey heavy Power Station boilers and heavy nuclear tanks. It had a very low floor, was long and made almost completely of steel.

It was to the end of stopping the shortages that I was employed on this day at Treeton Colliery. Demurrage could mount up considerably as days grew into months etc. This Manager was for keeping quiet about the surplus wagons to avoid this payment.

All Colliery Managers I knew ordered more wagons a day from British Rail than they required as an insurance, they thought, against not having enough and, to some extent, one could not blame them as each was responsible for his own Colliery and the output of that pit.

Treeton Colliery, which I had occasion to visit regularly, would not allow wagons to be placed into their empty sidings by British Rail Staff and the wagons would be kept on British Rail sidings at Treeton Junction. They moved the required number of wagons into their sidings using their own Colliery locomotive.

As a ploy to keep demurrage charges down, they claimed that trains of wagons placed in their dirty sidings required to be cleaned out before loading and they employed two or three men specially to clear the wagons of waste, such as flyash, or unwanted coal, say slack from a different Colliery. To avoid this payment, even for a day per wagon received, Treeton's Manager was happy.

They said that when a wagon left Treeton Colliery the quality of coal was precisely what was stated on the waybill, or on the wagon label, and was not of a mixed variety.

If it stated Power Station fine coal, then that was what it was. Again they had a point. Some Collieries were not so particular at cleaning out as Treeton.

If British Rail had to remove the waste or unwanted coal, there were certain places where it could be thrown out, mostly on to wasteland.

168. A vehicle must not be attached to any train Vehicles unsafe to if the Guard considers it is unsafe to travel, nor travel or must a wagon be attached to a train unless it is not properly labelled or directed in accordance with Rule 169. labelled.

169. Every loaded wagon must be labelled or Labelling of wagons. directed on both sides to its destination, with the exception of mineral traffic in train loads for journeys not involving marshalling during, or on completion of, the journey. When it is necessary for any empty wagon to be labelled or directed to its destination, such wagon must be labelled or directed on both sides.

Rules 168 and 169, about wagon labelling. From the BR Rule Book 1950, reprinted 1962, p. 169.

30. WAGON BESIDE ME ROCKED DANGEROUSLY

I found visiting the Steel Works most interesting. I had to look round all the firms' premises, including the 'sheds' where scrap metal and iron ore were taken out of the wagons by crane or hoist into vast 100-ton vats.

Of course, each firm, or Colliery, had their own internal wagons; in a Steel firm they would be filled with metal spillage or used by other traders to convey iron and steel. They were stencilled INTERNAL on both sides and they were knocked about more than British Rail wagons.

I had to make sure that BR wagons were being used for their lawful purpose, and this was not always the case. You would be surprised at what I found. One example I can give is that three places closely linked by rail were filling BR wagons with coal and other materials and passing them between each other's premises, treating the wagons as if they were their own.

When going into the sheds at Templeborough I wore a safety helmet specially supplied by the Steel firm. There were about 10 roads in the shed, each road holding about 25 to 40 wagons of differing sizes and shapes, mostly filled with scrap metal.

Overhead cranes dropped a magnetic disc into a wagon, metal of all shapes and sizes clung to the disc as it was withdrawn, to be placed in the vats before being transferred to an electric furnace.

As the magnetic disc moved over the roads, some of the scrap metal would become detached and spill on to the floor between Railway tracks and on to other wagons. On one occasion I watched the disc draw out of a wagon and, after it had passed overhead, began to walk past the wagon, intending to be clear of it before the disc again descended.

However, as I placed my foot forward into what I thought was a clear way between tracks, I found that I had stepped on what had been at some time or other a car door; car doors are never straight and this one, of course, was bowed and as I put my foot down it reared up on to my leg, giving it a sharp rap.

I winced with pain and, before I knew it, the magnetic disc had entered the wagon next to me, knocking its side and making it rock on its wheels. This gave me such a fright that I vowed never to walk through the sheds again. I never did. I looked in and counted the British Rail wagons within the shed and left it at that: I didn't want to be killed.

Safety was the rule for carrying cranes by train – no. 156, BR Rule Book, p. 164.

Removal of travelling cranes. **156.** (*a*) Before removing a travelling crane the person in charge of it must see that the jib is properly lowered and secured, and so fixed that it will clear the loading gauge, also that the balance box, and side stays where provided, are properly secured.

(*b*) When a travelling crane has to be conveyed by train it must, when practicable, be so placed that the jib points towards the rear of the train, and whenever possible the crane must be forwarded by a slow freight train.

(*c*) Before a crane is attached to a train the Station Master and Guard must see that the jib, balance box, and side stays where provided, are properly secured, also that the fastenings are in good condition, and the necessary match or guard wagons are provided. The Guard must, before starting, inform the Driver that the crane is being forwarded by the train, and at each stopping place on the journey the Guard must satisfy himself that the fastenings are secure. Wagon Examiners must also inspect the fastenings in addition to making the usual examination of the wheels, &c. If any defect exists in any of the fastenings, the crane must not be attached to a train, and, if travelling, it must be detached for the fastenings to be made good.

31. FOUR INSPECTORS CALL

Sometime after I had started work as a District Freight Rolling Stock Inspector, a certain person was appointed by the British Railways Board to the Divisional Manager's Sheffield Office to assist in the control of wagons in the area.

We were summoned to a meeting – all four Inspectors – by our office, the Wagon Control Office, where we were told that things were to alter and we would be working under this person's control.

He obviously had different ideas as to the workings of the rolling stock side of British Rail. In consequence instructions were given for all four Inspectors to make a comprehensive survey of the rolling stock within the Parkgate Iron & Steel premises at Rotherham.

There were six rail entrances and exits from the premises and, prior to this person's arrival, I had been told by my Head of Department not to approach the firm's Management before consulting him about anything I found out.

This, I was told by colleagues more knowledgeable than me, was because a high-ranking official of British Rail and a high-ranking member of Management in Parkgate Iron & Steel were big buddies of the golfing world. Whether this was so or not I don't know, but I had done just as ordered.

One Sunday at 08.00 hours precisely we four Inspectors arrived outside Parkgate Iron & Steel to carry out a complete census of all the BR wagons, sheets and ropes within its premises. Bill and Joe went in Joe's car as they had the greatest distance to cover. Len and I walked our section, which covered miles of sidings and tracks.

At the end of our census we found that there were more than 1,000 wagons within the firm's complex all owned by British Rail and also two wagons containing a full load of wagon sheets, the firm claiming on their 'standage' of BR property 600 wagons and had requested that sheets be provided the following Monday, when they had more than enough on hand.

It was arranged that we four Inspectors carry out this census every month in the future so that a true picture could be taken and true accounts kept on demurrage etc. Parkgate Management didn't like this and from then on always complained, saying that if we didn't stop this they would get more traffic to go by road.

When the computer Total Operations Processing System (TOPS) was adopted by British Rail, this gave a more accurate record, as all details of a train were logged on every occasion and the composition of a train or whereabouts of a wagon could be obtained simply by asking the computer.

Before TOPS a Central Wagon Authority was set up following the Beeching Plan and number takers were employed by British Rail to stand at the entrance to a firm's premises, especially large premises, to record the number of wagons inside. This to my mind was a hit and miss business, proved to be so by the introduction of the computer.

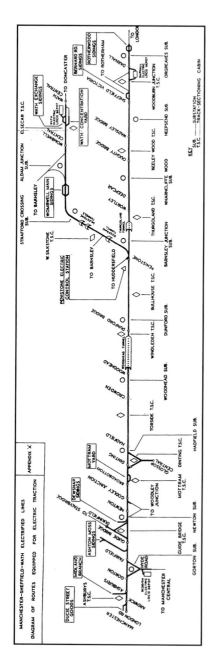

Above: a diagram of the Manchester-Sheffield-Wath lines, which were electrified in the 1950s, from Manchester-Sheffield-Wath Electrified Lines, Working Instructions, BR 29881, British Transport Commission, British Railways, Eastern and London Midland Regions, 1954.

Left: instructions about stopping for drivers of both electric and steam engines. From the same publication, p. 24.

20. Notice boards lettered "Electric Locomotives Stop Here" printed in white letters on a red background are erected at certain locations on running lines indicating to Motormen the points beyond which an electric locomotive must not run.

21. Drivers of steam trains when coming to a stand should, as far as possible, avoid stopping the engine with the chimney underneath section insulators or structures to avoid damage to this equipment.

After my time in the Freight Rolling Stock Inspectorate, I reverted to the Control Office at Sheffield, which had incorporated Rotherham Control Office. This was in Sheaf House, adjacent to the Midland Railway Station.

I was given a Rest Day Relief Controller's job, Class 2. Sheffield working practice was different to Rotherham's. In Rotherham Control Office two men were appointed to a Circuit, with one man being in charge and the other working under his jurisdiction.

When Sheffield Control took over, only one man took charge of the Circuit. Rest Day Relief Controllers had to learn – as usual in only three weeks – to take charge of Circuits and Relief Crew Controller positions.

I had to learn No. 1 Circuit, Horns Bridge to Beighton; No. 2 Circuit, Sheffield Midland Station and the route Tapton Junction to Barnsley/Holmes Curve (just South of Masborough); No. 3 Circuit, Beighton Junction to just short of Cudworth and Swinton/Wath Road where Doncaster/York Controls took over, Doncaster at Swinton and York at Wath Road.

I also had to learn the Relief Controller's job, which was Relief of Train Crews, allocation of Co-Co and Bo-Bo Crews and appoint these locomotives, electric overhead wire types, the Bo-Bo being for freight and having four wheels in front and four at the back, the Co-Co being a passenger engine and having six wheels in front and six at the back.

This was on the Wath-Guide Bridge-Manchester line via Penistone

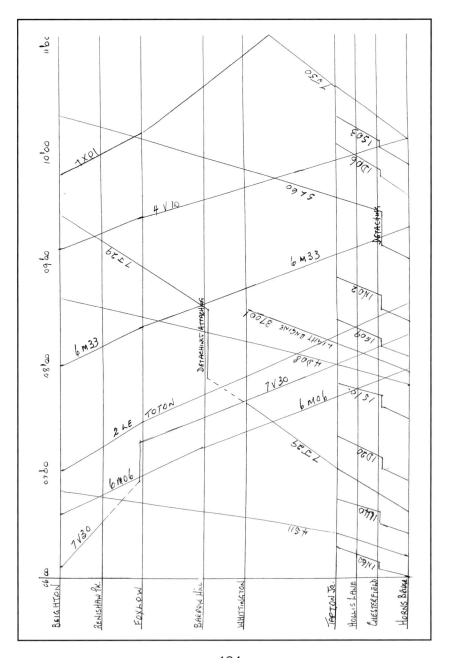

124

Author's note:

The graph (facing page) which I have drawn is not to scale and is just an example to show how a Controller received the passing or arrival times of trains from Signalmen. There is not the space to show the number of trains, banks and banks of them, one behind the other!

The graph itself was about 12ft long by 3ft wide, with rollers either side, rather like a scroll. The part not being worked on was rolled up out of the way.

On receiving a report, the Controller would draw a line from the last report of the train, eg Horns Bridge to Chesterfield, also Tapton Junction. Passenger trains into Sheffield went off on to the New Line via Dore and Totley. Trains going to Manchester via Stockport also went off the graph at Tapton Junction. The lines from Tapton Junction to Beighton were known as 'The Old Road'.

The graph was done in colour pencil: passenger trains were in green; freight trains on main lines were in blue, and on goods lines in brown; light engines (locomotive on its own) were in black on main lines, dotted black on goods lines; red meant the train was over its scheduled time at a station.

The train codes on the graph showed the type and speed of train (the first figure), its destination (letter after the first figure) and its number (last two figures). 1N60, for instance, was a passenger train (1) going to Newcastle upon Tyne (N), and its number was 60. J meant Sheffield District, D Doncaster District, V Western Division, X a Special.

125

and the notorious Woodhead Tunnel. This tunnel was very bad, foul, and wet, even after the line was electrified in the 1950s. When steam locomotives entered it their wheels began to slip, so to stop this sand from the boxes located near the loco's wheels would have to be placed on to the rail; steam would also be blown from the engine through little copper pipes in front of each leading wheel.

On one occasion in the days of steam a Driver had taken his train into the tunnel, travelling West in the Guide Bridge direction, and it came to a standstill when the loco wheels lost their grip. Smoke from the locomotives was tremendous in the tunnel and, if the train Crew could not touch the walls, they could lose direction. As happened in this instance.

On stopping, the Driver reversed the locomotive with the intention of sanding back a little way. When the wheels were skidding and you tried the sanding manoeuvre two or three times, you soon ended up disoriented. In the conditions he could not establish in which direction the train was going, and it ran back out of the tunnel straight into a newspaper train standing in Penistone Station.

I also had to learn the Locomotive Controller's position, which was monitoring the movements of locomotives working trains into and out of the Sheffield district. This monitoring was by drawn graph using coloured pencils. This position was subsequently withdrawn following my return to Doncaster Control in 1967.

There were two other positions as well: Relief cover for the Passenger Assistant and for the Deputy Chief Controller's Assistant. As I had knowledge of these positions prior to going into Sheffield Control, I was able to use this knowledge to good purpose.

33. JANET HAS CANCER

In the midst of this my wife, Janet, who was now teaching in a Special School, Anchorage, less than five minutes' walk from our home, was found to have breast cancer.

It was recommended that she should have operations for this, removal of the lump in her left breast as well as her womb and ovaries, and then have deep ray treatment.

All sorts of complications arose whilst she was in Doncaster Royal Infirmary, including infectious hepatitis, and every time I went there, something more drastic appeared to be happening.

After some weeks the surgeon at Doncaster Royal said Janet could leave the hospital. He advised her to take a holiday and then report to St George's Hospital, Lincoln, for radiotherapy and treatment by the heavy cobalt machine. The cobalt machine is not now used at St George's.

He said they had never given radiotherapy and the cobalt machine to a patient who had suffered from infectious hepatitis, but they would see how the treatments went. We had a week's holiday at Bridlington, John, Janet and I, then the following Sunday I took her to St George's.

For three weeks I took her to the hospital each Sunday, fetching her out each Friday, enabling her to be at home at the weekend. The radiotherapy and the cobalt machine were located in a concrete bunker with walls several feet thick.

It was a dreadful time; I was travelling to Sheffield every day, looking after John and the house, and so on, although I must say at this stage we had a lovely person, Mrs Edwards, to do most of the cleaning every Friday – she was a brick.

The Management at Sheffield were made aware of my problem and were very good to me, allowing me to work a day shift, thus enabling me to keep at work, look after John and, of course, go to see Janet in hospital regularly.

After she had received the treatment at St George's, Janet returned home to convalesce and to attend Doncaster Royal as an outpatient. At first it was one month between visits, then three months, six months, nine months and then a year. This went on for about five years before she was finally discharged.

When she started her convalescence, though, it would be about a fortnight before the Schools broke up for the annual Summer holidays. I approached the Welfare Officer at Doncaster, John Cobb, with my problem and, with his help, was able to transfer back to Doncaster Control Office in 1967.

The office was reshaped after Doncaster Control's incorporation of Lincoln Control. With three or four other Control desks and Relief Controller positions arriving in the office at Doncaster, the room was altered to accommodate these positions. It ended up with the Deputy's Assistant having to analyse more trains. Poor chap!

I took over a General Relief Controller's role, Class 2, which meant I again had seven different jobs to learn, including Assistant Locomotive Controller; GC Relief Controller; GN Crew Relief Controller; Diesel Unit Controller (monitoring such things as movements and failures); cover for the Deputy Chief Controller's Assistant when necessary.

But I was nearer home. To travel to Sheffield or Rotherham took me about one hour there and one hour back. Doncaster took me about a quarter of an hour and I could easily get home should the need arise to get there quickly.

Janet subsequently went back to her teaching duties when the Summer holidays came to a close and from then on had very little time off work for health reasons, apart from the check-ups.

Looking south from Doncaster station, the tracks on the right lead into the plant works where once Pacifics were built and the Deltic fleet was serviced. Photo taken by the author, 1999.

129

34. REDUNDANCY

A couple of years later a new system was adopted by British Rail, known as Maintenance Control. This brought Technical Staff from the Engineering side of the business into Control, causing redundancy to persons such as I, as they were, of course, technically trained in the building and working of diesel locomotives.

These members of Staff were to ensure that diesel locomotives were properly maintained and received their allocated maintenance examinations etc at their correct times.

Diesel electric locomotives had their A examination each day or, if for some reason this was not possible, the LD125 examination. Diesels were expected to be on the locomotive shed no more than two hours per day (the A exam took two hours, LD125 was shorter), as opposed to a steam locomotive which was on shed eight hours per day for cleaning its firebox and smokebox, oiling, filling its sandboxes, loading water and coal, and other maintenance.

In terms of maintenance one diesel was equal to five steam locomotives, according to British Rail Management.

It should be noted that diesel locomotives were subject to other examinations, each more extensive than the previous one: B, C, D, E and F. For example B was done every three weeks; the rest were carried out at certain strict intervals.

The final examination, F, was undertaken at a main maintenance depot and the cab was lifted from the frame and cleaned throughout, as was the frame. The chemicals used to clean the frame had to be such that, if any residue was left, it would not give off traces of gas which could cause a fire when the brakes were applied whilst the train or light engine, ie one without any coaches or wagons, was running.

From time to time major repairs had to be carried out and only designated depots such as Doncaster Plant Works behind Doncaster Station, Stratford in East London and Crewe did these, each one specialising in one or two types.

Doncaster, for instance, as well as carrying out coach and wagon repairs and building certain types of locomotive, did all the major repairs to the Deltic Fleet of passenger diesels, whilst these were in service. There were also Baby Deltics, which were not so powerful locomotives.

BR Management were to my mind correct in appointing Technical Staff to Control, as technical information had to be given to Drivers about difficulties experienced on diesel locomotives. For instance if a locomotive developed a fault, say a fuse had blown and difficulty had been experienced finding the fault, the technically trained Controller could advise on what and where it was.

These technically trained Engineers mostly were graduates. We didn't have the training which these men had and would have taken some time at University, for example, to obtain their skills.

70. Locomotive crews must keep a sharp look out for any unusual noises or unusual operation of the locomotive, including motors, gearing, bogies, pantographs or other equipment.
. . .

The Motorman must, if possible, isolate defective equipment with the least possible delay, and, if the locomotive is safe to proceed, continue the journey to destination.

Text from instruction 70, which shows why drivers of electric and diesel locomotives might need technical help. From BR's Manchester-Sheffield-Wath Electrified Lines, *1954, p. 52.*

Below: instruction 66, about the 'dead man's' safety device on electric locomotives. From Manchester-Sheffield-Wath Electrified Lines, pp. 50-51.

66. A "Dead Man's" device is fitted in **each** driving cab of an electric locomotive, operated **by** pedal at the **Motorman's** position or **by push** button on the other side **of the cab.** This **device** applies the automatic brake on the locomotive and the vacuum brake on a vacuum-fitted train and cuts off power 6 seconds after the pedal and button are released.

When a locomotive other than a disabled one, is in motion this device must always be kept operative and in no circumstances must the controller reversing key be placed in the "OFF", position, or the device rendered inoperative by any other means.

If the "Dead Man's" device fails, it must be cut out by closing the isolating cocks for the purpose and the Motorman must, if possible, work the train to the first signal box or station and there report the position, and await further instructions.

(*d*) Before a trolley is placed on the line, the Ganger or man in charge must, except as provided in clause (*l*), and as otherwise provided in clause (*n*), arrange for a Handsignalman to protect it. This Handsignalman must, except as provided in clauses (*e*) and (*f*), station himself ¾-mile, or such further distance as may be necessary, in the rear of the point where the trolley is to be placed on the line, to ensure the Driver of an approaching train having a good and distant view of his hand signal, and he must place on the rail 3 detonators, 10 yards apart, and exhibit a hand Danger signal.

The trolley must not be placed on the line until the Handsignalman is in position.

(*e*) Should the Handsignalman when going out to protect a trolley arrive at a signal box before he has reached a distance of ¾-mile, he must inform the Signalman what is about to be done and request him to keep at Danger his signals for the line about to be obstructed. The Handsignalman must place on the rail 3 detonators, 10 yards apart, exhibit a hand Danger signal, and remain at the signal box as a reminder to the Signalman of the presence of the trolley until the trolley has been removed or has gone forward ¾-mile from him.

Above: rule 215 (d) and (e), setting out the necessity for a handsignalman when trolley working – BR Rule Book, p. 241.

35. A NEW JOB IN THE ACCIDENT SECTION

I was made redundant from the Control Office at Doncaster in the April of 1969 and was appointed Clerical Officer Class 2 in the Signalling and Accident Section of the Divisional Manager's Organisation at Doncaster on 9th June that same year.

Within the Signalling and Accident Section was a team of Railwaymen who had special knowledge of Railway work. For instance, the Head of Section was a former British Transport Police Officer; the second in command was a former Signalman, as were two other members of Staff.

I had no previous experience in this type of work I was to undertake other than reporting major and minor incidents in the Control Log and working with others in the Control Office when accidents occurred.

However, I had a thorough knowledge of the Signalling side of the business and also the Operating side, ie all train working except the track (Civil Engineer's Department) and signals and telephones (Signal and Telecommunications Engineer's Department).

I had to learn the way that accidents etc occurring within the Doncaster Division were dealt with and reported. Reports had to follow laid down procedures and I was working under the Senior Accident Clerk.

Very often it was not immediately apparent what had caused the incident and it was then decided by the Divisional Management Committee that a Joint Enquiry would be necessary to clarify the details leading up to it, also to define the cause.

I was carrying out duties such as attending and reporting signal passed at danger Enquiries, what would often be a minor incident as opposed to serious incidents, such as deaths in train accidents or derailments.

It should be noted that sometimes a derailment could be a safety device. A train might stop on an incline near a junction and the Guard apply the handbrake in his brake van. If the Driver did not stop in the right place the train could start rolling backwards before the Guard could put the brake on, endangering other trains, crossings, and so on.

Therefore catch points were positioned at junctions which would cause the rearmost wagons or carriages to become derailed and halt the rest of the train. Catch points stopped many major accidents from taking place.

Sometimes a private firm's Staff were required to attend a Joint Enquiry. On one occasion a firm made arrangements for its Staff to recover scrap rails, timbers, etc, and they used a trolley on a British Rail line running to a certain Colliery.

A look-out man was to see that they worked in safety, being equipped with a red and a green flag, a horn and detonators to place on the line some distance away to warn approaching engines or trains.

However, the private firm's Staff did not wait for the Handsignalman and subsequently the trolley was struck by an engine and brake van going to the Colliery.

A member of the firm's Management was able to join the Enquiry Panel whilst his Staff were interviewed. He was also given a copy of the Panel's findings at the end of the Enquiry.

The major investigations were undertaken by the senior members of the section. I remember at Christmas time, about 1974, the Senior Accident Clerk had five Joint Enquiries to attend and report on – the chief one being of a Shunter who fell off a shunting pilot and lost an arm in the motion of the locomotive – and I had four.

When a major accident was investigated, the necessary reports of the Enquiry would be sent to Regional Headquarters at York, the Police, Area Managers, Depot Managers, and so forth.

Regional HQ would send copies to the Ministry of Transport, who would appoint their own Inspector to hold a Public Enquiry with all the relevant Witnesses, their Solicitors, Union Representatives, the Media. The Inspector would issue his own conclusions at the end of the Enquiry.

I had to investigate all aspects of Signalling, level crossings, fires on trains, eg from oil and dirt spillage on locomotive frames or from diesel locos' brakes being applied whilst a residue remained of the cleaning medium.

Other incidents included rock falls in cuttings, signal sightings (where planned road lights were tested for any confusion with colour signals), failures of the Automatic Warning System alerting Drivers to signals at caution, failures of the 'Dead Man's' safety device designed to halt the train if the Driver removed his feet from the pedal.

All were of differing characteristics and therefore it became to me a very absorbing job.

Northorpe, on the Gainsborough (Lincs) to Barnetby (Humberside) line, was notorious for derailments, especially to short wheelbase vehicles. It was a bad patch of railway track, as there were what is known as wet patches – water was present beneath the track and water can rise or fall, depending on the type of weather the area is subject to. These caused the Civil Engineer problems.

The Joint line, Black Carr (a few miles from Doncaster Station) to Lincoln via Gainsborough, also had problems which affected short wheelbase vehicles, causing speed restrictions to be imposed over this portion of track.

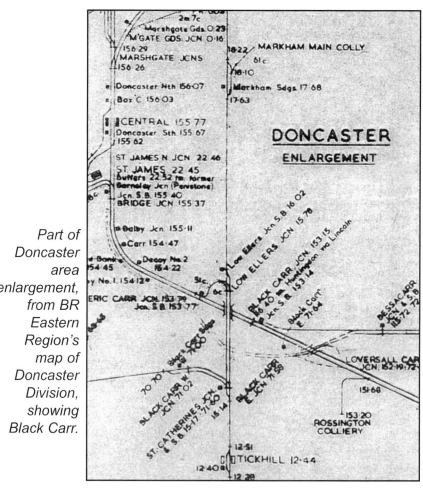

Part of Doncaster area enlargement, from BR Eastern Region's map of Doncaster Division, showing Black Carr.

Caution 1

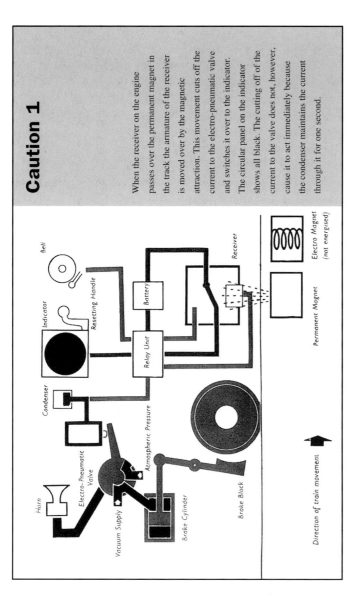

When the receiver on the engine passes over the permanent magnet in the track the armature of the receiver is moved over by the magnetic attraction. This movement cuts off the current to the electro-pneumatic valve and switches it over to the indicator. The circular panel on the indicator shows all black. The cutting off of the current to the valve does not, however, cause it to act immediately because the condenser maintains the current through it for one second.

The automatic warning system of the 1950s, on this and the next two pages. The diagrams show how the AWS acted when a train approached a signal at caution. British Railways' booklet, Automatic Warning System, is undated but said that by the middle of 1959 this system of the latest design was in operation King's Cross-York (188 miles), Euston-Rugby (82 miles) and Edinburgh-Glasgow (47 miles). The same year an extra 261 miles were being equipped.

137

Caution 2

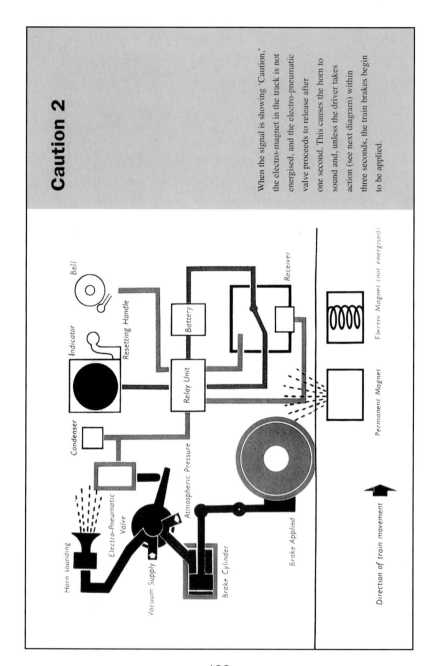

When the signal is showing 'Caution,' the electro-magnet in the track is not energised, and the electro-pneumatic valve proceeds to release after one second. This causes the horn to sound and, unless the driver takes action (see next diagram) within three seconds, the train brakes begin to be applied.

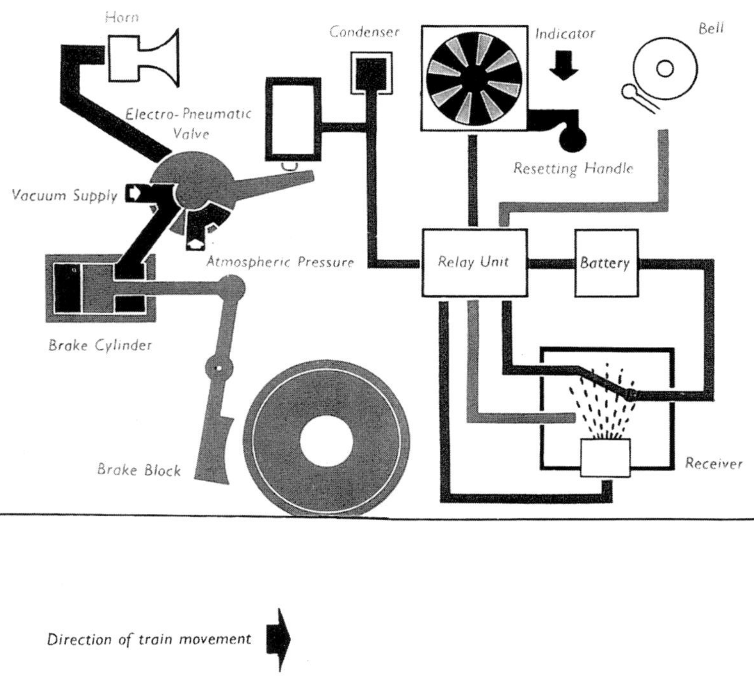

Resetting

On hearing the horn, the driver pulls the resetting handle and prepares to reduce the speed of the train by means of the ordinary brake handle. The moving of the resetting handle causes current to pass through the indicator again, making it show black and yellow in segments as seen in the diagram. This indication remains until it is cancelled by the action of the permanent magnet at the next distant signal (see Diagram *Caution 1*), as a reminder to the driver that he has passed a distant signal at 'Caution' and has used the resetting handle. The current also passes to the receiver, returning the armature to its normal position, and on to the electro-pneumatic valve, which closes, stopping the horn. If the driver does not pull the resetting handle until after three seconds have elapsed, and the brakes have been automatically applied, the valve in closing also releases the brakes again.

Bell

Indicator

Resetting Handle

Battery

Relay Unit

Receiver

Condenser

Atmospheric Pressure

Electro-Pneumatic Valve

Horn

Vacuum Supply

Brake Cylinder

Brake Block

Direction of train movement

In 1976 the Senior Accident Clerk at Doncaster left the Railway Service. I applied for his post and was appointed. This was a Class 3 post; in Clerical grades the higher numbers denoted higher grades, the opposite of the Supervisory grades in the Control Offices.

Being Senior Accident Clerk meant that I was responsible to the Head of Section and was to do the main work of investigating and reporting the more serious derailments, loss of life, collisions, etc.

Other members of the section reported on the minor incidents, such as members of the public falling on the platform and receiving slight injuries, barrows falling on to the track in station areas. Some incidents suddenly became serious although at first thought to be minor. These Staff also did the filing and so forth.

On arriving at work at 08.30 hours I would find a copy of the Control Logs on my desk, giving details of all the incidents which had occurred in the 24 hours commencing 06.00 on the previous day to 06.00 on that particular day, or in 48 hours over the weekends.

It would amaze the reader to have read the Logs, as they could vary in content and number of pages considerably.

Each day would be different because the same thing never seemed to happen twice. You might have two deaths on the same day, but each would be different. Derailments were often within a few feet of each other on different days, but the cause could be entirely different. I would never know what I was going to do in a morning. For instance, although there might be only five minor incidents in the Log, by 09.00 hours there might be a body found on the line at some point or there had been a derailment blocking the Main line or subsidiary lines.

The Control Office always notified the Emergency Services (Police, Ambulance, Fire Brigade, and so on) and made the necessary arrangements to divert rail services.

Control's job was to ensure that a full and detailed report was made by the train Staff, Shunters, Porters, Technical Staff, Engineer's Staff, and Signal and Telecommunications Staff. These reports would subsequently be forwarded to the Signalling and Accident Section and landed on my desk.

I collated all this information and, from the evidence submitted, prepared a full report which went to British Rail Management. Where necessary, I issued a directive as regards disciplinary action to be taken by the Area Manager, Depot Manager or other person in charge of the member or members of Staff at fault.

We were not allowed to take any reports from members of the public. The British Transport Police and the local Civil Police were responsible for these reports.

If there was to be a Joint Enquiry, I would be informed by the Management of the decision to hold it, where it was to be and who was to chair it. The Chairman was always the Divisional Operating Manager, later known as Operating Officer, *except* when a minor investigation was made into, say, a signal passed at danger with no subsequent accident occurring or an allegation of Staff behaviour causing trouble. Then a Divisional Signalling Chief Inspector would chair the investigation.

It was my job to liaise with the Chairman, agree who was to attend the Enquiry from the Operating side, contact the Heads of other Divisional Departments whose Staff were required to attend, such

141

as Civil Engineer, Signal and Telecommunications Engineer, and obtain assurance that their Department's Witnesses would be present, together with the name of the person they elected to sit on the Panel of the Enquiry, if it was not themselves.

At the investigation of a more minor incident, Inspectors of the respective Departments would represent those Departments.

I had to book a room where the Enquiry would take place, nearly always in Gresley House. However I have been at these Enquiries at Hull and Scunthorpe, the Area Manager's Office on each occasion, and at Newark and Doncaster Plant Works Boardroom on two occasions.

I also had to arrange for refreshments (cup of tea and biscuits) for the members of the Panel and the Witnesses.

Of course, a separate room had to be available nearby for the Witnesses to wait, ready for their appearance before the Panel, which could vary in size considerably, depending on the number of Departments concerned in the Enquiry.

For some time there had been talk that the Unions would attend all Joint Enquiries and near the end of the 1970s it was agreed with Management that the Union Organiser should be invited to attend Enquiries to represent the particular member – National Union of Railwaymen, Associated Society of Locomotive Engineers and Firemen, as the case might be.

The Union Organiser would be able to speak to his own member or members before the Enquiry and I always gave him, and indeed all the Panel members, a full, detailed report giving all known facts. No supposition was included and it was headed Preliminary Report!

The Union Organisers sat with the Panel but did not take part in questioning the Witnesses. They were allowed to talk to the Panel after their Union member had been questioned and had left the room. Discussion then took place.

I believe the Union Organisers were there to ensure that fair play was always paramount. Although at first I was not certain that this procedure would work, I can only say that the Organisers did make a contribution to the outcome of all the Enquiries I attended.

Doncaster Divisional Manager Mr Bleasdale presenting Geoff with a long-service (35 years) award – a pair of binoculars. Janet was also at the 1975 presentation.

37. WITNESS OBVIOUSLY WAS NOT TELLING THE TRUTH

The manner in which these Joint Enquiries were conducted was very fair to all Witnesses, as the Union Organisers saw, no matter whether the Witness could be described as 'good' or otherwise.

I only know of one case which I attended when one Witness was told to go home, think about the incident and write down what really did happen.

This was because under questioning he got to a point where he obviously was not telling the truth and was getting himself into a position where he was contradicting himself over and over again. Next day the Enquiry was reconvened, specially to get the man's statement absolutely correct.

The reconvening of an Enquiry often caused major problems. Members of the Panel, of course, were often Heads of Departments who had full diaries and this made life difficult for them.

It was also difficult for me, as I had to arrange rooms to be free where Witnesses could wait and arrange with the Witnesses' Depot for them to be released from duty again the next day.

When the Witnesses arrived, I had to make sure that all were present, check that they knew why they had been called to attend, tell them whilst their Union Organiser was present what was expected of them and their rights as far as being a Witness was concerned. I would take them to the Witnesses' room.

Of course, before this I had taken my recording instrument into the room where the Panel were to sit, arranged the desks and seating,

144

provided my Preliminary Report and also blank white paper to enable notes to be kept.

I acted as Clerk to the Court, as it were, bringing into the room each Witness as required, introducing the person to the Chairman of the Panel who, in turn, introduced the Witness to the other members of the Panel.

The Witness would be asked to make a statement as to the part he had played in the incident or following the incident, as the case might be, and I had to record this as he spoke.

The recording instrument in use when I entered the Signalling and Accident Section was a disc in the shape of an old record disc. The modern instrument, which used cassettes, was brought in in 1980 and was a big improvement.

It was placed on a desk where I could operate the hand microphone and be in a position to change the disc or cassette if necessary.

Any statement or part of the statement could be played back to the Witness if necessary, to ensure that facts could be checked and continuity maintained. Any misunderstanding would be revealed and could be amended.

Prior to the use of the recording instrument, Shorthand Typists had to take notes of what was said. This was very laborious as two Typists were required.

When a statement had been made and both the Witness and the Panel were satisfied with what had been recorded, the Chairman or another member of the Panel would question the Witness based mostly on his statement and facts which had come to light and were already known to the Panel.

Both the questions and the answers were recorded by me and

subsequently, when the Witness had been dismissed, I had to get the disc or cassette to the Audio-typist in the Typing Pool. This could be difficult as the Typing Pool was on the fourth, ie the top, floor of Gresley House.

If the Boardroom, also on the top floor, was free, the Enquiry could use that. But very often it was being used by other Departments and the Enquiry would be held on the first or second floor. Then other Signalling and Accident Staff were engaged to take the disc or cassette to the Typing Pool.

The final report of the Enquiry was written by me. The Operating Officer was responsible for the report and technically should have compiled it. However, I usually did it and then tendered it to the Chairman for his approval.

Gresley House, Doncaster. The Control Office was on the second floor, and Signalling and Accident on the third floor where Geoff's desk was beside the second window from the end, on the right. The private rail freight company EWS now operates from the building. Photo by the author, 1999.

146

During Ted Heath's Premiership new County boundaries were drawn in 1974 and new Counties made, one of these being Humberside, which incorporated parts of the former East Riding of Yorkshire and North Lincolnshire.

The new Humberside Fire Brigade requested British Rail to let them have all the nearest road access to rail points within the new boundaries. This, together with the Divisional Civil Engineer's Staff, we were able to do, giving all map references from the Ordnance Survey Maps. We gave farm access as well as road access.

About the time we supplied these map references, the Nypro chemical firm located just outside Flixborough, near Hatfield, experienced what became a very big explosion after a pipe ruptured and a cyclohexane vapour cloud ignited. Dozens of Staff within the firm's premises were killed or injured; also, outside the premises, damage to a considerable amount of property occurred.

Difficulties were experienced by the Emergency Services at and around Flixborough at the time of the explosion, and they all wanted a better response to an emergency, such as a train derailment.

To help to overcome the problems in future British Rail organised a mock derailment of a passenger train at Appleby, on the Stainforth to Brocklesby line. Appleby is three miles North-east of Scunthorpe and I believe it was chosen because of the level crossing, the topography of the line and the difficulty of space for the Emergency Vehicles – Ambulances, Fire Tenders and Police – to park.

It is obvious that Fire Tenders have to be in a position to use their hoses and other emergency equipment at an accident of this nature. Also that Ambulances have to be able to be near enough to rescue the injured and then go to the nearest Hospital, in this case Scunthorpe Hospital.

The staged derailment, Exercise Echo, was to take place one Sunday morning, 5th October 1975, and all the necessary Emergency Authorities were alerted about it, although the actual time and place were not made known to them.

I attended as an observer, making all the necessary records of the arrival of the Fire Tenders, Police, Ambulances, BR Staff, etc. These were taken in conjunction with a Police Sergeant, who also made a record of the happenings.

Many lessons were learned and caused the respective Emergency Authorities to overhaul their emergency arrangements, including having better information as regards accessibility to Railway property throughout the area.

From an observer's view, the Fire Brigade were the most impressive in their approach and actions, the manner in which they went about their business and the efforts made to release the casualty who was locked in the toilet of the derailed coach (dummy, of course), and the speed at which they worked, team work especially.

In addition, the Ambulance Service impressed me greatly and the Hospital Staff (Doctors and Nurses) gained my respect and admiration for the way they tackled the difficulties. They were up with the Firemen, having climbed the ladders, giving treatment on the spot, ie inside the toilet whilst hanging over the side of the upturned coach, assisting the Firemen to release the casualty.

As I had experienced previously when derailments occurred, the media, namely Television Crews with their aggressive 'I'm here and

I'm filming' attitude, I found to be a nuisance and did get in the way. The Television Crew had somehow climbed on to the upturned coach and were endeavouring to film the Firemen and Hospital Staff getting the trapped casualty out.

They didn't seem to bother that they were actually in the way of the rescue teams as they coped with the situation.

Who to tell in the event of an accident – no. 177, BR Rule Book 1950, reprinted 1962.

REPORTING OF ACCIDENTS

177. When an accident to a train, or an obstruction, or a failure of any part of the works affecting the safety of the line, occurs, the next station or signal box open on each side must be immediately communicated with by the most expeditious means to enable Drivers and Guards of approaching trains to be advised of the circumstances, and assistance to be obtained if necessary.

All accidents or obstructions must be reported promptly to the persons indicated in the appendix to the working time table, an advice being sent by telephone in the case of serious mishaps.

In the case of personal injury the names and addresses of witnesses and the injured persons must be obtained.

The stations where the starting of other trains is liable to be affected by delay caused by the accident or obstruction must be immediately advised.

173

149

39. PRESSURE POINT AT PEASCLIFFE

Following the introduction of the 125 mph passenger trains over the East Coast Main line, two problems arose, causing British Rail quite a lot of trouble.

First, when passing another train or other trains at speed, especially in tunnels and even when going into or out of tunnels, ballast lifted up between trains and the glass windows on some of them were broken.

Most of these incidents occurred when the 125 mph trains were passing, approaching and coming out of tunnels near Grantham: Peascliffe Tunnel, a few miles North of the town, and Stoke Tunnel, to the South.

The pressure within these tunnels when two such high-speed trains passed each other was enormous. I actually drew graphs for the Management, indicating the position and point where the incidents occurred, from times passed to the Control Office from signal boxes along the route the trains travelled.

Suitable action was taken by British Rail to minimise the problem and eventually this kind of difficulty subsided considerably. For example at both tunnels the track was lowered to accommodate the larger and higher Continental vehicles being brought into the country.

The second problem was more serious. I know of one incident in the Newcastle Area, two occasions in the Doncaster Area and two occasions in the King's Cross Area where trains travelling at speed became divided; the most serious case was near Yaxley

(Peterborough). A Doncaster Driver sent to our Signalling and Accident Section a report to the effect that, whilst he was travelling on the Up line, the leading locomotive of a 125 mph train on the opposite (Down) line passed his train, the rear portion of the other train following some quarter of a mile behind, still travelling at speed.

Because of these problems British Rail had to redesign the 'buckeye coupling' on the 125 mph trains, so that the Shunter, or whoever was involved in the coupling, could easily see that the 'tongue' had dropped into place, ie engaged properly. This could not be seen before the redesign.

It should be noted that the first 125 mph trains ran on the old Great Western lines before they were introduced on the old Great Northern, or East Coast Main line. The difference between these Railways was that the distance between the Up and the Down lines was as follows: Great Western 10 feet; Great Northern 6 feet.

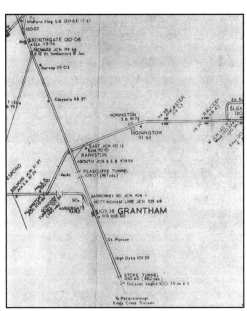

Problem tunnels Peascliffe (north of Grantham), and Stoke (south of the town), the start of Doncaster Division. Enlarged section of BR map of Doncaster Division.

151

40. CLERK TO 150 ENQUIRIES

During 14 years in the Signalling and Accident Section at Doncaster, I attended 150 Joint Enquiries at which I acted as Clerk to the interviewing Panel.

In addition to these, I had to investigate on average 25 deaths per year which had taken place on British Rail premises. Each death was investigated separately from British Transport Police, although we did liaise with both the Transport and Civil Police.

However, the co-operation with the Civil Police was very limited. They were mostly very remote and we did not get much detail from them, although this was subsequently given to us by the Transport Police after they had liaised with the Civil Police. Liaison between them was, as I know, on a good basis.

As with Civil Police and procedures, Transport Police would not give us access to their Witnesses' statements, but we would give them certain information that had come to light in our investigations.

If a body was found on the line, the Police attending would act in a very different manner. The Transport Police would act according to British Railways Board Regulations and mark the place where the body was found, take all necessary details on the spot, then have the body removed so that the passage of trains would be resumed. All trains would automatically be stopped over the track where the body was found until it had been taken away.

The Civil Police would not allow the passage of trains until their Photographer had taken photographs etc and their on-the-spot enquiries were completed. As the Photographer was not always immediately available, this could be some time. We, as British Rail Personnel, hoped that the Transport Police would arrive first on the scene to enable traffic to run again as quickly as possible.

Joint Enquiries were always the directive of the upper Management but they were a must for any derailment of a passenger train, death or injury of a passenger travelling on a passenger train and death or injury when struck by a train. Trespassers were often the ones who were found to be dead or injured on the line.

At one place in Lincolnshire, Rauceby, about two miles from Sleaford, over a period of time we had several deaths of outpatients at a Mental Hospital. What the Hospital Authorities did to reduce this I do not know, but the Local Authorities must have known the difficulty surrounding these deaths.

The number of suicides that I had to investigate at this location was more than normal, even for Railway suicides.

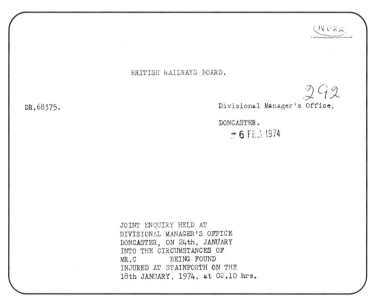

The front page of a joint enquiry report – this one about the case of Mr C (next chapter).

BRITISH RAILWAYS BOARD.

DR.68375.

Divisional Manager's Office,

DONCASTER.

- 6 FEB 1974

JOINT ENQUIRY HELD AT
DIVISIONAL MANAGER'S OFFICE
DONCASTER, ON 24th, JANUARY
INTO THE CIRCUMSTANCES OF
MR.C   BEING FOUND
INJURED AT STAINFORTH ON THE
18th JANUARY, 1974, at 02.10 hrs.

Location

Stainforth Station is situated on the Barnetby (Wrawby Junction) to Doncaster (Marshgate Junction) line at 06 miles 40 chains. Stainforth Junction signal box is situated at the West end of Stainforth Station Down Platform and is partly electrical and part mechanically operated. The points and signals at the East end of the Station are controlled by an electrically operated Panel, the points and signals at the West end of the Station being mechanically operated.

The signal box is staffed on a three shift basis by 2 Signalmen and 1 Train Recorder on each shift.

The Signal Box controls the junctions at each end of the station, i.e. the line to and from the Hull direction and the junction to and from Applehurst direction.

Track Circuit Block Regulations apply on the Down and Up Main lines between Scunthorpe and Stainforth signal boxes, also on the Up Hull line between Thorne Moor and Stainforth signal box.

Absolute Block Regulations apply on the Down and Up Main lines between Kirk Sandall Junction signal box and Stainforth Junction signal box and on the Down Hull Line between Stainforth and Thorne Moor, also on the Down and Up Branch lines between Stainforth and Bramwith Station signal box.

Permissive Block Regulations apply on the Down and Up Goods Lines between Stainforth Junction signal box and Kirk Sandall Junction signal box.

The signals are of the colour light and semaphore types.

The Signalmen on duty at Stainforth Junction on the night of 17th and 18th January 1974, were Signalman E   working the Panel, Signalman M   operating the mechanical frame, Signalman B   acting as the Train Register Recorder.

Stainforth Station is staffed by a Porter between the hours of 0600 to 2100 hrs. each weekday except on a Thursday when the afternoon Porter finishes at 2200 hrs, the extended time is for the payment of wages. On Thursday 17th January, the Porter left duty at 2200 hrs.

Train Details.
2D95 21.40 Doncaster to Cleethorpes, D.M.U. train comprising, P/C 50040 - T/C 56040 - P/C 50002 - T/C 56011, worked by Driver N.R. H   of Grimsby and Guard A   of Cleethorpes.

Incident.
On Friday 18th January, 1974, at approximately 02.10 hours, Signalman B   at Stainforth Signal Box, heard a cry from outside the signal box, he brought this to the notice of his colleagues in the Signal Box and, as it was thought that a drunken man was roaming outside, Yard Chargeman B   was requested by telephone to make an investigation, Signalman M   , leaving the signal box also to investigate.

Shortly after leaving the signal box, Signalman M   found a severely injured man laying in the 6ft. between the Up Goods Line and the Through Road, the mans head was near the Up Goods Line, the lower part of his body towards the Through Road. M   returned to the signal box to request that an ambulance and Police be called to attend, the necessary B.R. Personnel were also informed and attended.

Enquiry reports followed a format, starting with the location, train details and a description of the incident. This is p. 1 of the report concerning Mr C. Full names are omitted at the author's request.

One or two Joint Enquiries stand out more than others. The one that I found to be the most memorable was where a member of the public, I will call him Mr C, was found injured at Stainforth Station, near the Up Goods line.

He was discovered at 02.10 hours on 18th January, 1974. One of the Signalmen heard faint cries for help and telephoned the Yard Chargeman or Supervisor to ask him to investigate. Another Signalman also made a search and found Mr C.

He had one leg severed below the knee and the other leg was severely injured. His spectacles, false teeth, trilby hat and shoes were lying near him; his small suitcase was found further away along the Goods line. The Ambulance and Police were quickly on the scene and he was conveyed to Doncaster Royal Infirmary.

The incident as reported to Doncaster Control Office appeared on the 24-hour Log, which I found on my desk at 08.30 hours on 18th January.

The item read that Mr C had been found and the only ticket on him was a BR ticket from Hastings to Durham. How then had he been travelling to Stainforth, AND WHY? As Mr C was traumatised and unconscious, these questions could not be answered immediately.

After reading the Log from the Control Office, I had to go to the Gents' toilet and, on entering, was asked what I was worried about by one of the Passenger Office Staff, Keith. I told him that he would be worried if he had read the Log that morning and then told him about Mr C.

155

"Strange you should tell me of the BR ticket," Keith said. "My mate was in the Down side Refreshment Room last night and was speaking to a fellow from Hastings."

"Where does your mate work?" I asked.

"In Accounts," he said.

On returning to the Accident Office I contacted the Accounts Department and spoke to Keith's mate, who told me about the short conversation he had had with the gentleman in the Buffet, also giving me a description of him.

The person he had spoken to was small, wore a brown trilby hat and an overcoat, and carried a small case. This description tied in with the description given by the Staff at Stainforth.

I quickly got in touch with the British Transport Police Inspector and gave him this information. He then questioned the Bar Staff in the Refreshment Room on No. 5 platform. Because the Staff on the station had been on the afternoon shift, the investigation was really a problem. However, progress was made when they came on duty.

It was learned that Mr C had been drinking McEwans and barley wine and subsequent investigation revealed that at some period he left the Refreshment Room to talk to a Driver and Guard in the Down side waiting room.

A search was made to identify the men concerned and they were subsequently found. Both men were interviewed by the Police and their written reports to their Depot Manager were sent to the Signalling and Accident Section.

Both stated that a small man in a trilby hat had approached them in the waiting room. His speech was very impaired and he swayed as he stood so they had difficulty in making out what he said; however, they finally found out that he wanted to know when the train to Stainforth would leave the station.

They told him that the next train was booked to leave at 9.40 pm and Mr C then went back to the Refreshment Room.

Later, when the diesel train was standing in the bay, the Guard who had been in the waiting room saw Mr C being helped on to the train by a Station Supervisor, who had found Mr C trying to get into a front coach, which he could not do as the first two of the four cars were locked. The Guard told Mr C to sit nearby and Mr C sat immediately in front of him.

Eventually the train left Doncaster Station and, as it was a pay train, the train Guard came to Mr C for his fare. The waiting room Guard, who was travelling home to Scunthorpe, assisted Mr C to get the correct fare from the loose change in his pocket.

During the journey the Scunthorpe Guard noted that on the seat beside Mr C was a suitcase which had a label with 'Hastings' as part of the address.

When the train arrived at the Up Main line platform at Stainforth, en route to Grimsby and Cleethorpes, Mr C had to be assisted from the train by the two Guards.

The idea was to take the highly intoxicated man off BR premises. However, after being conducted to the footbridge steps on the platform, Mr C decided he wanted to urinate. By this time the train was 19 minutes late and therefore both Guards decided to leave him to make his own way over the footbridge, and the train then left shortly after 22.00 hours.

Mr C was therefore on BR premises from that time until found at 02.10 the next morning. What had occurred during this period was not known. Further investigation of Crews on all 28 trains that had

APPENDIX 'A'.

Name.   C   B
Grade.   Relief Signalman, Class 1, Scunthorpe.
Date of birth.
Date entered
        service.
Date entered
    present Grade.

STATEMENT OF WITNESS.

On 17th January, 1974, I took duty at 22.00 hours at Stainforth Signal Box,
prepared for an 8 hour shift. I had previously had my prescribed rest period
before taking duty. The shift continued normally until at approximately 02.10
hours I heard cries coming from outside the signal box. When I drew the
attention of my colleagues to this, Signalman M   left the signal box and
discovered an injured person lying on the Up Goods line. I notified Doncaster
Control and requested an ambulance and the Police to attend.

Q.   When the 21.40 Doncaster to Cleethorpes train arrived at
            Stainforth did you see this particular train arrive ?

A.   I would normally have seen this train arrive but I cannot
            recall whether I did or not on this particular occasion.

Q.   And you have no recollection of seeing anyone on the Platform
            after the train had left the station ?

A.   No.

Q.   Can you remember anyone wandering on the station or in the
            vicinity of the track within the following few hours ?

A.   No, not until we heard the cries at 02.10 hours.

Q.   Were the cries fairly faint ?

A.   Yes they were fairly feeble, I heard it first and I drew the
            attention of my colleague to it.

Q.   What happened then please ?

A.   Signalman M   said I'll go and have a look outside and took
            and hand lamp with him to investigate, I then contacted the
            Yard Supervisor B   for him to examine outside looking
            for a drunk as I thought it may be a drunken man at this time.
            When M   had been outside only a few minutes I heard him
            shout that an ambulance was required, and I went on to the
            telephone to Control Doncaster to request the attendance of an
            ambulance as an accident had occurred. I then went to the
            window of the signal box and T   shouted 'he has got a leg off'

*Example, from the Mr C report, of a witness statement
and following questions. Full names and other
identifying details are omitted at the author's request.*

passed through Stainforth Station between those hours revealed that only one Driver of a light engine had actually seen a man on the Up platform about 23.15 hours, but could not give a very good description of him.

The locomotives of the five trains which had passed over the Up Goods line were examined. However, no traces of blood or human tissue were found on any of them. We therefore had nothing to prove which train could be involved.

It subsequently was found that Mr C was on his way to a funeral at Durham and had decided to break his journey and go to Stainforth, where he had previously been a very active Miners' Union member.

He had known the area intimately and therefore, to shorten the walking distance to the village, instead of going over the footbridge to leave the station he decided to take the unauthorised route via the coal yard, a long-standing practice of some passengers.

He would have to go across several Railway lines and lines in the yard – where local Coal Merchants had their bunkers, into which wagons would be offloaded – then climb a wooden gate in fencing.

I was later informed that £200 was found to be missing when Mr C was able to be interviewed by the Police.

It turned out that, arriving at Hospital, Mr C had been undressed and an item of clothing, in which the £200 was placed, had been burned: being in strings and fouled by oil and blood, it had been put in the incinerator.

42. BEST WITNESS OF ALL, A KING'S CROSS GUARD

Another incident that occurred which I found interesting was when a passenger train travelling from Leeds to King's Cross was discovered to be on fire in the vicinity of Black Carr and Loversall Carr, a few miles from Doncaster Station. Fields on either side of the line were also on fire, as they were set with corn.

A coach wheel journal (which holds the axlebox in place) had collapsed due to it becoming white hot because the axlebox ran short of grease whilst the train was travelling. Railway Staff had not noticed this.

Eventually the whole of the frame of the journal disintegrated. This often caused a derailment, although it did not do so in this instance.

Debris from the shattered journal was found scattered along the line and in the fields, after the Fire Brigade had put the fires out. The journal pieces looked fossilised, pitted with small depressions.

This had fooled the Fire Chief from York HQ, who thought that carbon from the diesel engine exhaust had fired the fields and not any other cause. However, very rarely has this caused lineside fires, unlike sparks from steam locomotive funnels. The Chief Mechanical and Electrical Engineer at Doncaster knew what to look for and walked the line himself, discovering the evidence.

What surprised me was that the Guard of the train, who was actually as black as coal, was the best Witness I ever had. He gave me a statement from the time he had signed on duty at King's Cross, all the details of taking over the Leeds train, such as making sure all the coaches were fit for the journey, and also the taking over of the return Leeds to King's Cross train. This, of course, was the normal practice; what was not normal was that he gave me all the correct commas, quotes on, quotes off, semi-colons, etc: truly a very professional and highly educated man.

I personally thanked him for the way he gave his evidence.

188. In the event of a fire occurring on a train Train on fire. the undermentioned arrangements must be carried out:—

Trains conveying passengers.—The train must be brought to a stand immediately the Guard or any member of the staff travelling on the train becomes aware of the fire, unless he can take adequate steps to promptly and completely extinguish the fire. If he is in any doubt as to his ability to extinguish the fire the train must be stopped. He must, however, avoid stopping the train on a viaduct or in a tunnel, or other similar unsuitable situation.

209

If fire broke out on a train . . . rule 188 (above and right), BR Rule Book 1950, reprinted 1962.

Rule 188

The Guard, and any other members of the staff who may be travelling on the train, must take all practicable steps for the safety of the passengers and assist in their detraining when necessary. Every endeavour must also be made to extinguish the fire or to prevent it spreading to other vehicles.

If the train is not protected by fixed signals, protection in accordance with Rule 178 must be afforded by the Fireman or, in the case of trains or engines the driving cabs of which are single manned, by the Driver, after he has satisfied himself that the fire is being dealt with.

Other Trains.—The train must be stopped as quickly as possible but must not be brought to a stand on a viaduct, in a tunnel or in any other unsuitable situation, and prompt steps taken to endeavour to extinguish the fire or to prevent it spreading to other vehicles. If the train is not protected by fixed signals it must be protected by the Guard in accordance with Rule 178.

All trains.—If necessary, in order to prevent the fire spreading to other vehicles, the vehicles in rear of those on fire must be detached, the burning vehicles drawn forward at least 50 yards, uncoupled and properly secured, the leading portion drawn ahead to a safe distance thus isolating the burning vehicles.

210

161

43. ROAD LIGHTS V SIGNALS TEST

The Signalling and Accident Section was also the Department that arranged for signal sightings to be made. This was to ensure that any road lights being positioned by the local Council in the vicinity of the Railway line were not mistaken for Railway signals.

The Council would advise the Railway Authorities of their intentions and the Signalling and Accident Section would be informed of when the lights were to be switched on.

A special Signalling team was composed of Locomotive, Driver, Secondman (Fireman), Motive Power Inspector, Divisional Operating Inspector, Signal and Telecommunications Inspector, and they would be instructed to travel over the section of line where the new lights were positioned and to report immediately to the Control Office whether or not there was conflict.

Sodium lights, giving a yellow or orange light, also other types of lighting giving a blue or green light, could make life difficult for any Driver of a train, should conflict occur, and thus it was essential that these tests were carried out. In some cases, Council-owned lights had to be relocated.

The sun, which at times of the year lies low in the sky, was also a difficulty and, although hoods were placed over the top of the colour light signals during Winter months, it has been known for all three or four aspects of signals to appear to be lit.

This always seemed to take place in the Grantham area round about February. The hoods could not be lowered or the Drivers would not be in a position to see the proper signal aspect. Drivers were instructed to stop at such signals and report the position to the signal box concerned and to await instructions from the Signalman.

The Signalling and Accident Section also arranged for speed checks of trains. Speed restrictions were and are imposed over certain sections due to conditions of the line.

For a number of years a speed restriction was in force over Bawtry Viaduct between Doncaster and Retford because of the rail conditions at this point. It was subsequently made safer and the restriction lifted, saving five minutes on the journey time.

When the Civil Engineer made an allegation that trains were running too fast over a section of line and there was the possibility of accidents, derailments, etc, a speed check was made. Two Operating Inspectors would be instructed to take a wooden box, containing electrical equipment, to where the checking of speeds was to take place.

One Inspector stayed with the wooden box, the other went further along the line, able to see the first Inspector and also to make a note of the locomotive number and type of train, noting any hand signals from the first Inspector indicating that the train was indeed travelling faster than authorised. Later the speed gun, the same as the one used by Police to ascertain the speed of cars and lorries, was used, and I believe is still used.

Drivers who exceeded the speed limit were disciplined. Those taking their trains five miles or more above the limit would lose workdays and therefore pay. Their record would be endorsed each time. If speeding became in any way consistent, the Driver could be taken off driving duties permanently.

Another example of speed restriction was that in force on the line between Doncaster and Kilnhurst on the way to Sheffield because this section was subject to falling sand and stone, being in a cutting.

Speed would be monitored once or twice a month, not at regular times as Drivers would then know when it was to be done.

I once went to a derailment which had taken place near Tickhill, not far from Doncaster, due to a speed limit not being observed. The train of about 35 wagons, containing coal en route from Colliery to main Power Station, became derailed where the Railway line ran high past farmers' fields, the elevation from fields to track being somewhere about 40 to 50 feet.

Only about eight wagons remained on the track, the rest lay all over the banking, spilling out the coal. To make it worse, there were about six inches of snow on the ground.

It was my job to obtain all the numbers etc of the wagons and, to do this, I had to go down the banking and look at the labels on the side of the wagons. Putting my feet down, in my Wellington boots, I would go about two or three feet into the snow-covered coal and it was a very difficult thing to do to obtain the wagon details from the side of the wagon.

Details on the labels which had to be recorded for the investigation included information such as when the wagon was last in the workshop for repairs. When the Total Operations Processing System came into being, all the details of the train were in the computer and it became unnecessary to take desperate measures, as I had to do on this occasion.

Eventually I found myself at the bottom of the banking in a farmer's field. It was impossible to climb the banking, so I set off to walk across the field, parallel to the Railway track. Then I came to a stream, about six feet across but I did not know how deep; part of it was covered in snow and ice.

For a moment I was stuck and then I noticed that the boundary fencing was fragile and loose at one end. I hesitated and then made my mind up to climb to the damaged fencing, endeavouring to get over the stream in this way. Thankfully I made it without falling in, but it was absolutely hair-raising.

The train Driver admitted that he had forgotten the speed restriction on this section of line and, as the sun was shining, was enjoying the beautiful views. He was, of course, disciplined in respect of his failure.

It is ironic that two Drivers could sign on for duty at the same time, to work two different trains, and that the outcome of their day's work could be so different. One would be rewarded financially for reporting a broken rail on the opposite line to the one on which his train was travelling, thereby avoiding a derailment; the other passed a signal at danger – a very serious offence for a Driver – and, of course, he was disciplined.

This actually happened and was recorded: two Drivers on duty, same time, differing circumstances.

Part of BR Rule Book no. 35, from the section on fixed signals, p. 30.

(iii) Subsidiary signals in the form of disc signals, or of the banner type with red or yellow arm in a circular frame, or position light signals, or semaphore signals with small arms or colour light ground signals—the Normal indications being:—

By day	*By night*
Red disc.	Red light or white light.
Yellow disc.	Yellow light.
Red arm in horizontal position in a circular frame or on a white disc.	Red light, white light or the day normal indication being illuminated.
Yellow arm in horizontal position in a circular frame or on a white disc.	Yellow light or the day normal indication being illuminated.
Position light signals with one red or yellow light on the left and one white light on the right, in horizontal position, or no lights.	Same as by day.
Small red semaphore arm, or small white semaphore arm with red stripes, in the horizontal position.	Red light, white light, or no light.

165

In November 1983 I retired from British Rail, having completed 44 years and two months' Railway service. I had decided to take the early retirement settlement offered to me.

It was envisaged that the Divisional Management Organisation at Doncaster would be made redundant and that most jobs, including the one I was doing, would be located at York, 35 minutes' journey by rail each day, there and back. At the same time Sheffield DMO went to Leeds.

This I did not fancy doing, and myself and several other long-service personnel made our minds up to retire.

Looking back over that period, I enjoyed what I did throughout my Railway life, although in the Second World War when bombs and shrapnel were a very present daily event working on the Railway, especially at night, was not a pretty thing to be involved in. Whilst I was at the North box at Nottingham Victoria Station life got a bit hairy at times.

I rather think I took what opportunities came my way. I studied and obtained three Railway Certificates for train Signalling and Operating procedures, etc. I also took an O level in English at Night School at the age of 47 and received a Certificate for the same.

To fill in a little of the domestic side that I have largely omitted so far, my father died in 1950.

They told him at Ransom that his life's work was finished, they could do no more for him and he would have to leave, to move into a

Council house. My aunt, my mother's sister, who had a guest house in Skegness, said: "Spend a week with me. Forget all about it."

There was a visiting Preacher at the Methodist Church and my father went to hear him. He returned, and that is when he had a heart attack and died.

But my mother went into the Council house, a little bungalow in Mansfield, where she stayed until her death, from heart failure, in 1965.

Ransom eventually became more of a heart-lung Hospital, I believe, tuberculosis being practically wiped out, then a Hospital for people with learning disabilities. Now it is the headquarters of the North Nottinghamshire Health Authority whilst the site round about is a business park.

During the period 1966 to 1983 Janet and I had a caravan, first for travelling over long distances, John, our son, and Pat, our poodle dog, being with us. But some two years after travelling about to various places, we decided to have a static caravan at Sutton-on-Sea, which is between Mablethorpe and Skegness on the East Coast in Lincolnshire.

When going on to the beach I had the job of throwing Pat's ball, then kicking John's football – Pat was marvellous at running and catching a ball in mid-air.

We thoroughly enjoyed caravanning and we had a number of friends at the caravan park. We spent holidays there and it also got us away at weekends, away from our work.

We would come back home on a Sunday night, having spent from Friday night at the caravan. We were the first people to be located on the site, which had water and electricity laid on, with showers in the toilet blocks.

Later, about 1981, we had a new caravan with all mod cons built in, eg shower, large gas stove and large fridge.

Of course, having free Railway passes, we were able to go on the Continent and see how the other people lived, travelling to France, Spain, Holland and Switzerland.

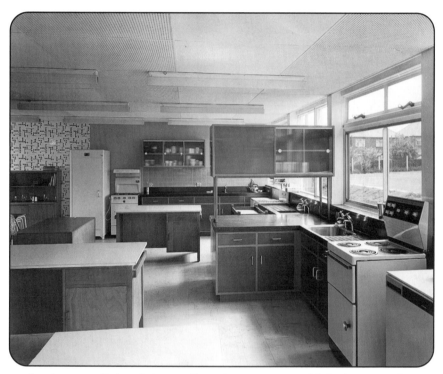

Anchorage School domestic science room which Janet took over in 1965. Pupils were taught to do practical cooking, for example, breakfast, dinner, tea. Janet made work cards showing a picture of the meal, utensils required (such as egg cup, spoons, saucepan) and method. The cards were covered by a kind of clingfilm so they could be used again and again.

Janet continued to teach at Anchorage School; the Education Authority did not want her to retire as she was too valuable to them.

I in the meantime kept house, doing all the work, washing and cleaning, etc, cooking the evening meal. I also began to write this book.

In October 1984 Janet retired at the age of 60 and, by this time, John, our only child, had been at Reading University, obtaining his BA Honours Degree in History in three years, and having another two years' study to enable him to get a further degree.

He was researching for a Doctorate, his thesis was the life of Lord Clarendon. Halfway through his studies, however, it was found that an American researcher had touched on his thesis and this stopped him getting a Doctor of Philosophy Degree.

After one year's study at Nottingham University for his Teacher's Certificate, John was given a History teaching appointment at Thomas Lord Audley Secondary School, Colchester, Essex. Whilst there he completed his thesis and was awarded his Master of Philosophy Degree by Reading University.

He also married a Colchester girl, Carolyn, who is a Supply Teacher, and they have three children, Emily, Miriam and Joseph, who are now aged 12, 10 and six respectively.

We therefore looked round for a property in the vicinity of Colchester and subsequently found one at Lawford, where a new estate was being built. We fell in love with a three-bedroom detached house on the hill that we subsequently bought. The views from the back windows were really great. We could look straight on to the fields and woods which form part of the Constable Conservation Area which, of course, comprises the area of his paintings, including Flatford Mill and The Hay Wain. Before other houses were built across the road from us we could see the River Stour.

Manningtree Station is just five minutes' walk away and it is easy to catch a train to London or Norwich; Harwich is about 14 miles away, Colchester and Ipswich 12.

We sold the house in Doncaster and the caravan at Sutton-on-Sea and took up residence at Lawford on 20th December, 1984.

On the second day after we moved in the Methodist Minister arrived, inviting us to attend his Church. Then the Rector of the Parish Church of St Mary, Lawford, arrived and invited us to go to the Church. We discussed various things, our plans, and so forth, and within days he asked us to hold a coffee morning for other new arrivals on the estate. The idea was that people coming into the area would quickly get to know each other and make friends.

He made it his business to meet all new arrivals and invite them to his Church. He was a lovely man and we willingly took up his plan to create a good spirit in the estate.

We began with 10 ladies. Over a period of eight years members came and went but about 40 ladies (most were retired) and two gentlemen (both retired) either came to or held coffee mornings every other Wednesday; religion and politics were taboo subjects for discussion.

When the estate was in its early days, five residents died within a couple of months or so, leaving their wives widows, with no other means of making friends than the Churches or our coffee mornings.

I joined the Stour Choral Society, which is based at Manningtree, and am still an active member. We rehearse in Manningtree Methodist School room each Monday evening.

Over the years the 60 or so members of the Society have sung all types of religious and classical music, and have also been in partnership with the Kantorei Choir, from Frankenberg-Eder, Germany.

Partnership means that we exchange Choir personnel. We have been to Germany on two visits to the members of their Choir and they have had return visits here. They sing in a Lutheran Church with a high roof which gives a wonderful acoustic effect. The friendship has been a great success throughout.

Both Janet and I became members of Acorn Village, a community which enables people with a learning disability to lead as full a life as possible. It is a charity and is located on the Clacton/Harwich road at Mistley Hall, about two miles from Lawford.

We helped with fund raising, events with stalls and suchlike, and musical events. Subsequently we had to withdraw our membership as Janet had a recurrence of the breast cancer and had to have a mastectomy in 1993, and another in 1995.

We also volunteered for the Meals on Wheels service, conveying dinners to the elderly and disabled for six years. We had to give that up when Janet became ill.

Our son, John, joined Colbayns High School at Clacton as Head of History after a couple of years at Thomas Lord Audley School. At the moment he is Head of Sixth Form at Colbayns.

We went to Belgium, Germany and France with John whilst he was Head of History, when he took children and parents to the battlefields of the First World War, eg Vimy Ridge North of Arras,

171

Tyne Cot at Passchendaele, giving us all the necessary details and interesting things that had occurred.

We also visited First World War Cemeteries and the Second World War Cemetery at Dunkirk.

John at Degree Day, Reading University, 6 July 1985, when he was awarded his MPhil.

46. VISIONS AT ELY AND CHELMSFORD

Two other highlights during our retirement are to my mind extraordinary.

In August 1986, together with two friends, we went to Ely Cathedral for the first time. One has to pay a fee to enter and to have a look round. Whilst being on my own at the rear of the Cathedral, I prayed for world peace and, in so doing, I saw what appeared to me to be an ancient doorway.

The door opened and I saw the figure of a monk or hermit without his cowl; he looked directly at me and I noticed most vividly his white hair. This vision lasted for about a minute, then the door closed, leaving me quite bewildered as to what had really happened.

Following this vision I noticed nearby an iron stand where candles were lit; other candles were there which visitors could obtain and light. I selected one, lit it and then placed it on the iron stand, having paid a very low price for it.

I mention this now as it really shook me. How would this vision affect me?

The other thing happened towards the end of September, also in 1986. During the morning of the 29th, I said to Janet: "Let's have an early lunch and go by train to Chelmsford." This we did, arriving at Chelmsford at approximately 13.10 hours.

To go to the town centre from the Railway station, one has to walk down a main road with a number of Estate Agents' shops. We looked at quite a lot to see what the local prices of houses were; we were shocked by the high prices and congratulated ourselves on buying our delightful house at Lawford.

As we walked down this road we came to a notice which indicated that the Cathedral was close by. We had not seen this on our only previous visit to Chelmsford; however, we approached the South door, which I found to be heavy, and I therefore pulled it open so that Janet could make her way through the aperture. I then followed.

Janet, as usual when visiting a Church, went to where the books and icons were for sale. I, on the other hand, just stepped inside the door and saw right in front of me what I would describe as an almsbox. It was quite big and not unlike a house on stilts.

I put my left hand into my trouser pocket, with the intention of giving some money for the upkeep of the Cathedral, when I happened to look across it for the first time and just froze.

There are two bronze pulpits in the Cathedral, either side of the Chancel steps; I could not see beyond these from where I was standing, but behind the pulpit furthest from me, just behind a pillar, there was the most wonderful person I have ever seen.

He was clothed in a pure white habit; the cowl was down and he had the most wonderful gold and auburn hair, cut like a monk's but without the dome on the crown. In his right hand he held a sword and he brandished this three times, swinging his arm in a circular motion. The last time he brought it against his face, the blade raised upwards, the hilt of gold against his chin.

He then stretched out his left hand and I noticed his wide sleeve. At this time a basket of hot coals, the basket being in the shape of a crown in wrought iron, moved from the pulpit nearest me towards his outstretched left hand.

174

He caught the stem of the crown of burning coals and stood there. At no time did he directly look at me.

I turned away and said involuntarily: "Oh no!" On entering the Cathedral the last thing I expected was to see something of this nature. But when I looked back I noticed that the vision was still in the same position. I felt that he knew everything about me and I could do nothing about it.

Whilst still standing near the offertory box, I saw what I can only describe as a long, buff, cardboard screen coming towards me from the vision and on the screen was this notice in black letters:

I am come with sword and with fire to purify the earth.

The vision then vanished and I noticed two women just a little distance away from me; they were talking about the roof of the Cathedral. From where they were standing I am sure they could not have seen the vision I had seen.

One other thing that impressed me was that the vision never looked directly at me and I am thankful that he did not do so, as I did not think I would have been able to withstand the gaze. He had the most healthy face I have ever seen.

From that time I have been convinced that God is, Jesus Christ is and the Holy Spirit is. One God World without End. To be sure, I was brought up by my parents to believe in God and the vision was only to convince me more.

In addition to the previous enterprises we embarked on when we moved to Lawford, we were members of Manningtree Methodist Church, taking great delight in singing with members of other Methodist Churches at Mistley, Bradfield and Ardleigh who always assisted us at special occasions.

Rene, our organist, brought a number of people from our Church together and we gave concerts to the elderly and others. We formed The Manningtree Methodist Melody Makers to give these concerts.

Often as we were performing sketches and singing to the elderly and disabled who were in nursing homes we seemed to have more fun than our audience, who either listened or slept throughout some concerts.

Rene died some two years ago and nothing has been the same; there is now no-one to organise the concerts.

In 1987 I became a Lawford Parish Councillor and was on the Council for 12 years, retiring in May 1999. I was the oldest member.

There were a few things that I was unable to get Essex County Council and Tendring District Council to do something about. At times it was like banging one's head against a wall. However, we were able to do some good, I hope, within the parish.

For example we had a problem of disposing of domestic waste. We badgered the County Council to provide facilities to have garden and building waste disposed of, using an area of land for skips to be loaded. These skips had to be taken to Colchester land waste disposal site. This, of course, cost money but with a grant from the County Council and by charging motorists 60p to transport their waste into the skips we just about broke even.

As a Council we were able to look at plans submitted by Householders, Farmers, Limited Companies, etc, to Tendring District Council, the Planning Authority for this district. We then gave an informed opinion as to whether we agreed or otherwise with the plans.

Policing and security of housing were discussed with the local Police force. Transport within this rural area was also discussed with the respective agencies, ie bus company and Railway officials.

As previously stated, my brother, Bill, died on the Burma-Siam Railway. My sister, Gertrude, had kept up with the Royal British Legion concerning the Prisoners of War and the efforts being made to visit their graves.

In 1995 the Legion's Pilgrimage Department got in touch with my sister and I, as they were hoping to be able to visit the Allied Prisoner of War graves at Cemeteries including Thanbyuzayat, Burma, where Bill was buried, and were enquiring who was prepared to go on a 12-day tour of Thailand and Burma (or Myanmar as it now is).

As my sister was not at that time in good health, I consulted Janet, my wife, and decided that I would like to go, and indicated this by letter. The tour was to take place from 21st January to 1st February, 1996. It was specially mentioned that there was only a possibility of going to Thanbyuzayat Cemetery, as it was within territory which was subject to rebel forces and no tourists had been allowed to visit it since its completion some 50 years ago.

On 20th January, 1996, I went to the Union Jack Club near Waterloo Station in London to meet the other Pilgrims who were to go on the tour; also to stay the night, have breakfast and then go together to Heathrow Airport to go to Bangkok on the Thai Airways International Boeing 747 plane.

In the morning, when we were to go to Heathrow, one of the 52 Pilgrims had a heart attack. The British Legion Doctor and Nurse who were to accompany us attended to him and he was not able to go with us.

We actually visited all the places listed on the tour. When I returned home I wrote an account of the visit, which I trust the reader will find interesting.

Part of Thanbyuzayat Cemetery, kept clean and beautiful by the War Graves Commission, with Burmese help. Photo by the author, 1996.

48. PILGRIMAGE TO THAILAND AND BURMA

We spent two days at Bangkok. The first day we visited the Grand Palace, where the Royal residences and the venerated Chapel Royal of the Emerald Buddha are located.

The second day we visited the Commonwealth War Graves Commission Cemeteries at Kanchanaburi and Chungkai, and held services there. Relatives attended their loved ones' graves.

When leaving Heathrow we took with us a large number of red poppies in wreaths and sprays and these accompanied us throughout. At each Cemetery we attended persons who had relatives buried there were able to place a spray or wreath on these graves.

We then joined the train at Ban Pong Railway Station, which took us over the River Kwai Railway Bridge, thence over the rail line which clings to the side of mountains; the line passes over a great viaduct which curves two ways in a huge S bend.

The journey was of one-and-a-quarter hour's duration. We sat on wooden seats with the windows down. There were draughts everywhere but as it was so hot no-one complained. Photographs were easily taken and light refreshments were a relief – small cakes and pastries like any at home, plus iced water, lemonade and cups of tea.

When we got off the train at Wang Po Railway Station, Saiyok, Kanchanaburi, we rejoined the two buses that had originally taken us to Ban Pong and then travelled back to the River Kwai Restaurant, right near the bridge. There we had a very enjoyable

Thai lunch of meat and fish with rice and a fruit sweet, followed by beer or soft drinks.

After lunch we went to the nearby Jeath Museum, which is in a building of bamboo and attap, the actual type of building in which Allied PoWs were housed. A bamboo shelf was situated some two feet above the earth in the sleeping quarters – 21 inches wide per man of thin strips of bamboo strung together with dried leaves.

Exhibited were photographs of Prisoners of War in various poses with Japanese guards. Emaciated bodies of PoWs were seen; cruelty and starvation were clearly visible. It was a greatly moving scene to behold. Original drawings by Prisoners were also shown.

We then returned to Bangkok by bus. On 24th January we left for Rangoon (or Yangon), Burma, by air bus, with an Australian Pilot and Malaysian Co-Pilot.

Ban Pong station, Thailand. The locomotive, Japanese, worked on the Burma-Siam Railway and the foreground rail tracks were laid by Allied PoWs. Author's photo, 1996.

180

49. RANGOON RECEPTION

After getting our keys at the Summit Parkview Hotel we had a wash and brush-up in our rooms, then we again joined the buses to go to the Official Reception held by the British Ambassador, Mr Robert Gordon OBE.

We entered the Ambassador's Residence and were received by the Ambassador and his wife. We then went into the garden, where the Reception was held. Lights on the Residence itself were on, whilst to the delight of everyone small coloured lights were scattered in the trees which surrounded the lawn.

We were royally entertained, being served with iced drinks and pieces of celery and other suchlike vegetables to dip into delicious sauces etc.

About 9 pm we adjourned to the Golden View Restaurant, which certainly lived up to its name and where we had a meal of rice and vegetables, sweet and sour pork, and so on, beer or soft drinks. Whilst eating we were entertained by Burmese dancers, who did their special dances, emphasising the hand and finger movements to Burmese music.

At the end of this the Management of the restaurant gave each member of the Pilgrimage group a present which turned out to be a specially designed native bag for shopping, beautifully embroidered. These were particularly acceptable.

In addition one lady member, whose birthday happened to be that day, was given a 'tiara', which would not be out of place at any High Society Concert, and a lovely bunch of flowers. I don't know how the

Management came to know it was her birthday; none of us knew. Eventually we went to our hotel and bed.

The next day, 25th January, we drove about 34 km to Taukkyan War Cemetery for a short service and wreath-laying ceremony.

Following this we again lunched in a restaurant and then visited the site of the old Sittang River Bridge which was blown up by the British forces as they withdrew towards the Arakan region, where they finally made a stand against the Japanese Army.

We returned to our hotel via the coastal route, noting that the inside of the peasant huts (made of bamboo and attap) were lit only by one candle. Outside most families had a fire on which a black pot was positioned, obviously cooking the evening meal.

Wang Po station, Saiyok, Kanchanaburi, where the group left the train after travelling along the Burma-Siam Railway from Ban Pong. The teak sleepers (on the right) may have been used on the railway from the start. Author's photo.

50. BILL'S RESTING PLACE AT THANBYUZAYAT

We awoke early on 26th January as we were to fly East to Moulmein (now Mawlamyine) Airport in a turboprop-type aeroplane, due to leave Rangoon Airport at 7.30 am.

However, although we were 45 minutes early for the flight, we were informed that there was a heavy mist at Moulmein and the Pilot would not leave until the weather had improved.

The sun was pretty high in the heavens when at 8.30 am we joined the aircraft and some half-hour or so later we touched down at Moulmein, being greeted by young Burmese ladies who welcomed us with two red roses per person.

Standing near the airport were two air-conditioned buses which would take us the 64 km to the War Cemetery at Thanbyuzayat where my brother was buried with other Allied Prisoners of War. No party from Britain had been able to reach this Cemetery for 50 years due to the political conditions within Burma. We were conveyed to the Cemetery, three trucks of fully armed Burmese Soldiers in the front, three trucks of fully armed Burmese Soldiers in the rear.

It was not explained to us at this time that the Burmese Authorities had informed the Ambassador the previous day at 7 pm that the visit to Thanbyuzayat was 'off'. The Ambassador, with the Foreign Office, took tough action with the Burmese Authorities, which resulted in them changing their minds. We heard that Britain said it would ask nations providing money or other help to cease this aid.

At 10 am the sun was very high in the sky, there were no clouds whatever, the heat was intense.

Bill's grave (middle one), a poppy on the front. The Royal British Legion Standard Bearer Mr Peter Potton stood with Geoff behind the grave, Mrs Potton taking the photo.

A Cross of Sacrifice is positioned at all the Cemeteries we attended and we held a service at each Cross. The service at Thanbyuzayat was conducted by the Archbishop of Rangoon, assisted by an Australian Priest, with other Church dignitaries. The British Legion were represented by members in their Uniforms; the Standard Bearer, Mr Peter Potton, had led the way to the Cross.

Wreaths were placed by the Ambassador and Legion members. Prayers were said and two hymns sung, 'Oh God, our help in ages past' and 'O valiant hearts'. This was followed by Trumpeters of the Burmese Army sounding the 'Last Post'.

After the service, which was very moving, relatives (widows, brothers, sisters and so on) were able to go to the graves. There are 3,771 burials at this Cemetery.

I quickly found where my brother was buried, on the back row of Block B1 – Row O, 10th grave; the Legion had supplied the Pilgrims with maps giving the exact location of loved ones' graves.

I was able to place a spray of British poppies on Bill's grave, plus the two red roses which I had received at the airport and a small cross of remembrance also supplied by the Legion and brought from Britain. Mr Potton, the Legion's Standard Bearer, stood beside me behind the grave whilst his wife, Noreen, took our photographs.

All this was a very emotional experience and many tears were shed. We spent two and a half hours at the Cemetery and I was able to take a number of photographs of it and the area round about.

Following this we were escorted to Setse Beach only a few miles away where we had lunch right on the beach at a restaurant owned by the Burmese Government. It was rice etc as usual; as far as I was concerned the food was not much different to the meals we had had in Thailand. In the afternoon we journeyed the 24 km to visit Amherst (now Kyaikkhami) to view the Kyaikkhami Pagoda.

This was very large, built on a hill, as most pagodas are. The interior of this pagoda was lavishly decorated.

All the large pagodas are so heavily covered with gold leaf and other costly metals, such as white gold and silver, as well as mother of pearl. The elaborate decorations on the buildings were actually breathtaking.

It became too much for me. I could not understand why these buildings were decorated so lavishly when the ordinary people were so obviously poor. Even children as young as one and a half to two years old would approach us with their hands out, for us to place money in.

Give money to one child, then there would appear about 20 more. Where they came from I don't know, but it was difficult not to give something.

Thence to our Rangoon hotel.

Part of the River Kwai Railway Bridge, Thailand, a diesel locomotive hauling passenger stock. Author's photo, 1996.

A service was arranged in Rangoon Cathedral on 27th January, specially for the members of the Pilgrimage, conducted again by the Archbishop and fellow Clergy. Wreaths were again placed by the Ambassador and the British Legion.

The choir, all being Burmese, sang for us 'The Lord is my shepherd' (tune Crimond) in English. This service was also very moving and the 'Last Post' was again sounded by the Burmese Army Trumpeters.

Following this service we were able to visit Scott's Market, a native market about 100 yards from the Cathedral and now called Bogyoke Aung San Market.

To visit a foreign market is always an event. To visit this market was really something. One could buy all modern clothes, pottery, sweets, carvings, iron work; also parts of motor engines, accessories of all kinds. Nothing like Halfords; these were all in parts one never sees in Britian. We kept very close together so we did not get lost, as the market was spread over quite a large area. There were walkways between stalls and cross-pathways running directly opposite one another.

The Burmese Shopkeeper or Stallholder was very keen to get one to buy. One had to bargain to get anything reasonable. One lady member became quite good at this, so a number of us asked her to do the bargaining and thereby secured an article for less than we had hoped.

We also kept together because the Shopkeepers and Stallholders soon approached when you stopped to look at their wares. Two or three at once tried to get one of our group of 15 or so to buy their goods.

At night we went to visit the Shwedagon Pagoda, which was a spectacle as the buildings within this area of land are beautifully decorated with, again, gold, silver, white gold, blues, greens and rose colours, highly brilliant to see. We then had dinner at the Golden View Restaurant once more.

On 28th January we went by air to Mandalay, having breakfast on the flight. The journey took about three-quarters of an hour but we had to wait about an hour and a half in the airport before entering the aircraft. We experienced some long waits at airports.

We toured Mandalay, including the reconstructed Royal Palace (lovely teak woodwork and carvings), which was burned out in 1945, and Mandalay Hill. Lunching at the Honey Restaurant, we then continued by two Japanese air-conditioned buses to Sagaing, an ancient capital, now a Buddhist Pilgrimage Centre.

Finally we had dinner at the Pyi Gyi Mon Restaurant, which is built as a Royal barge. This was lit up at night and looked beautiful on the lake, which is surrounded by a wall one mile square, built, we were told, by Burmese prisoners, ordinary prisoners, not Prisoners of War. The inevitable rice, sweet and sour, etc, but this was most enjoyable.

The next day, following breakfast at our Mandalay hotel, we journeyed about two to two and a half hours by bus to the Ava (now Inwa) Bridge, one of the best I have ever seen. Road vehicles pass on the left and right of the bridge, and through the middle trains are able to run.

Standing on the bridge you saw overloaded road vehicles with men and women clinging to the rear and sides. It really was amazing.

188

However, I didn't see any road rage anywhere. Then we went to the old British hill station of Maymyo (now Pyin Oo Lwin), site of a Jungle Training School in 1941. A considerable number of colonial-style buildings remain.

We also went to the botanical gardens in Mandalay, where we found the grounds to be well laid out; the two lakes were seen and the pure blue from the reflected sky was something to be observed. It was ideal for photography.

On 30th January we went by bus to Amarapura, site of an ancient Royal city which now houses one of the largest monasteries in Burma. To the South of this monastery is Lake Taungthaman, which is spanned by the three-quarter-mile U Bein Bridge, constructed two centuries ago entirely of teak planks.

In the afternoon we flew to Rangoon, where we spent the night and had a farewell dinner in the Royal Hotel, which overlooks the Shwedagon Pagoda.

We had what was called a free morning on 31st January, which meant we could either go to Scott's Market again or to the National Defence Services Museum.

I went to the market, where I got a few things for my relatives back home. For my daughter-in-law I bought a long piece of cloth, the type that Burmese people hang over their shoulders; two parasols for my granddaughters and a suit for my grandson, a type of top and trousers. It was too big for him but he grew into it. He's nearly out of it now!

We departed from Rangoon by air to Bangkok and spent a few hours in the Bangkok Airport Hotel, where we had a buffet meal in the hotel gardens prior to catching our plane back to Britain. In all it was a successful Pilgrimage and tour and well worth making, even though the elderly people at times became tired!

Janet,
at her
home in
Lawford,
Essex,
about
1996.

Janet was born on 14th April, 1924, in Sutton-in-Ashfield. When she was an early age her family of mother, father and two brothers, George, 10 years older than her, and Alan, nine years older, left to take up residence in Hucknall, about eight miles North-west of Nottingham. Her father was an Insurance Agent for the Refuge Assurance Company.

Janet attended local Schools in Hucknall and left at the age of 14. For a time she worked at Ford's, a Nottingham haberdashery and clothes, etc, firm. Finally she was appointed Receptionist at Messrs Richard Lunt's Warehouse in Hounds Gate, Nottingham.

This firm had various departments, including clothing, baby clothes, and household commodities. She had to record everyone who entered the premises, help them to find the department they needed and be as helpful as possible to everyone within the premises.

The family moved to Carlton about 1938 and Janet continued to live a very sheltered life up to the time she voluntarily joined the Land Army at the age of 17.

However, she was invalided out four years later when she was 21 after falling through a nursery greenhouse roof and landing on a beam, breaking two ribs. She went back to work for her old firm, Richard Lunt's, and was married from there.

The lives of shift workers' wives are very hard and during my time as a Railwayman, over a period of about 29 years, before I joined the Signalling and Accident Section, Janet had to be on her own for many hours at all hours. When I was working 12 hours, especially on Relief Signalman's duties, it very often meant I was away from home 14 hours because I had to travel to the place where I was to work, and travel back.

While we were living at Rainworth, at Mrs Revett's, my cousin's husband, a Director of Messrs Lewis & Co, Nottingham hosiery manufacturers, thought up a scheme for Outworkers to be employed because of a shortage of women labour.

It should be noted that the war had just ended and it meant women were still in the Forces and therefore this caused difficulties with women labour.

Janet at once took on the work with other members of the community and, though the pay was nothing to shout about, and was subject to the amount sent and the amount done, they continued with this for quite a few months.

The work mostly was for women who were married and confined to the house because of children and because Rainworth was a Colliery village, their husbands being on shifts; it meant that they could earn themselves some pocket money.

The work entailed cutting the link strands from socks and other types of hosiery; socks were the predominant article. These came off the machine in a 'string of socks', or whatever – cotton or wool strands held them together. The work was not heavy but one had to be careful not to cut the foot of the sock. Janet spent about two to three hours a day on it, as far as I remember.

The hosiery came in large boxes, a certain number of items per box, and had to be carefully packed when they had been sorted properly.

Later we moved from Mrs Revett's and lived with a Miner and his wife. Whilst we were there, Janet was taught by a friend to do smocking, this being a form of decorative stitching on little girls' dresses and blouses. Janet was always brilliant with a needle.

She and the Miner's wife worked for a firm that made women's and children's clothes and they had to collect the garments that were to be smocked from a place at Mansfield, bring them home, smock all the garments in the boxes, then take them back to Mansfield.

If I remember rightly she was paid twopence (old money) per line stitched; again this payment was not a lot, although it helped to swell our weekly money and enable us to live a little better.

In 1949 we took residence in Mansfield Woodhouse at No. 3 Albany Drive, our first house. We had not a lot of money to use on ourselves, so Janet went to the Technical College at Mansfield two or three afternoons a week to learn how to make herself dresses and so on and was awarded three Certificates (by the East Midland Educational Union examination board), all First Class, two for Dressmaking, and one for Ladies' and Children's Tailoring.

Whilst at the College she was asked to take up teaching at a School in Rainworth, which she at first was loath to do, stating that she was not qualified enough. However, the Nottinghamshire County Council Needlework Adviser, Mrs Walters, assured her that she would only be teaching very young children one half-day per week.

The Lecturer had proposed to Mrs Walters that Janet was a good prospect for teaching young children. Some people have a special knack for teaching: patience, ability to pass knowledge to another and a personality that encourages pupils to higher achievement. Janet had all these attributes and the Lecturer obviously had noticed them.

Having been at the Technical College for about two years, Janet decided to further her knowledge by joining a Course for Technical Teachers in Dressmaking and Needlework at Clarendon College of

Further Education at Nottingham. This meant that she had to travel to Nottingham three times a week morning and afternoon and continue to travel to Rainworth for the half-day to teach the Junior School children elementary needlework.

Getting to Nottingham meant taking a bus from our house at Mansfield Woodhouse to Mansfield, about 10 minutes, and then taking another bus to Nottingham, about an hour. Getting to Rainworth also meant two bus rides and the total journey was only about 15 minutes shorter.

All this travelling was extremely hurtful to her as she had a claustrophobic condition and had to have tablets, which she took all her life, to enable her to travel.

Janet travelled to Nottingham three times per week for about five years and obtained her City & Guilds of London Institute Certificates in Dressmaking, Advanced Dressmaking and Needlework, again all First Class, and, in 1955, her City & Guilds Technical Teacher's Certificate, also First Class.

She was at this time teaching one half-day per week, a total of one and a half days, at three Junior Schools: Rainworth, and York Street and St Edmund's, both in Mansfield Woodhouse. She also taught over-School age students at Mansfield Folk College and was teaching at two Night Schools, held on Day School premises.

Clarendon asked Janet to take over the Needlework Class but we had our son, John, then and she was not able to do this. However, she returned to teaching at Night School when he was six weeks old; he was born on 13th July, 1956.

In 1958 we moved to Doncaster, where I had been appointed Assistant Controller, taking up residence at 3 Canterbury Close on John's second birthday. When we arrived, Janet approached the Doncaster Education Committee Representative who was in charge of Night Schools with a view to starting Evening Classes. In the interview which followed, this person asked her: "What have you got that others haven't? I've been trying to get Night Schools started with others and I have failed."

Janet assured him that she would post notices through every letterbox on the estate, with the information that a Night School would open, giving the date and other details. The response was spectacular: 40 women on the first night for Dressmaking and Needlework with some Tailoring. To begin with the classes were two nights a week; later it became three nights per week.

The Education Committee Representative could not believe it; however he, with others, kept asking her to do more, which eventually became impossible.

Janet continued to teach at two Night Schools and also taught Dressmaking and Needlework at Doncaster Technical College. Then she went into Day Schools: Wheatley Girls' High School, a temporary post, followed by Rossington Girls' Secondary School, a permanent position. This School eventually merged with the Boys' School. To finally teach at a Day School full time was the culmination of many, many hours of hard work and effort.

If John needed looking after at all, sometimes I was able to do so when my shifts were convenient; at other times Joan, a neighbour's girl who was taking her O and A level exams, was a great help.

In 1964 vacancies arose for Teachers at a new School very close to where we lived. It was to be a Special School for children with learning difficulties.

Janet applied for the post of Domestic Science Teacher and was appointed. Anchorage School was officially opened in 1965 but in 1966, as previously stated, Janet was found to have breast cancer and for a period of about four months life was terrible for all of us.

After successful treatment she continued as a Teacher at Anchorage.

Subsequently she was given a sabbatical year to attend Sheffield University, where she studied Sociology, Psychology and Child Development and received the Diploma in Education. For this course she had to travel by car to Sheffield every day during the terms – 20 miles each way.

On receiving her Diploma, she was asked to organise a School near Scawsby which was to be a new venture. There was a Centre for people who were mentally handicapped where those over School age were able to do some light craft work. Those of School age and thought not to be educable were more or less looked after by Hospital Assistants.

Janet was asked by the Education Department at Doncaster to take on the job of setting up an educational establishment for those of School age. This change, which was Government policy, required Staff to be trained for teaching where teaching was possible, to order the necessary books, toys and equipment, and so forth.

This was quite a job where some of the children were kept in crib-like beds for their own protection. Some were incontinent and others had various difficulties controlling movement.

Janet organised the change. She declined the position of Head Teacher, preferring to return to her teaching duties at Anchorage School. She knew that her talent was to motivate children with learning difficulties and help them and their parents to cope with these difficulties.

About a year later Janet was appointed Deputy Head Teacher at Anchorage, becoming the only woman Deputy Head in the West Riding of Yorkshire. On four occasions she took over the Headship, once for a year whilst the Head Master went to Leeds University for his Master's Degree. During this time a new Diagnostic Unit was constructed and brought into use, and a learner pool was built in the grounds.

At the Diagnostic Unit children from the age of two and a half to eight years could be monitored by the Teacher and Staff appointed to the unit. Some children were autistic, some were subject to fits. Practically all had behaviour problems. A special room adjacent to the unit had a two-way mirror so that any particular child could be watched and monitored.

Anchorage then became a split-site School, five miles between the sites; the age groups were two and a half to 14 years at the Lower School, and 15 to 19 in the Upper School.

During the 1984-85 Miners' strike Janet had to travel between sites by car and was stopped every day by Police looking for secondary pickets.

Later in 1984 she started a well-earned retirement.

In 1993 and 1995 she had mastectomies to both breasts and died in March 1999.

Janet had been a very dedicated Teacher and her courage over 33 years of living with breast cancer was amazing. Cancer is a very insidious disease and, although physical, becomes a constant mental difficulty. We had many a crisis to overcome; anything unusual became a serious situation as the mind tends to go immediately back to the cancer.

This is very difficult to overcome and throughout the 33 years no Medical Authority suggested counselling of the mind. Indeed Janet made her own search for help through books etc. The main two books she kept right from 1966 to the end of her life were 'The Miracle of Mind Dynamics' by Joseph Murphy and 'Your Thoughts

Can Change Your Life' by Donald Curtis. These books she took wherever she went. Other books were obtained throughout the 33 years, all on healing and the mind.

Our doctor had told Janet quite frankly: "You've got two months to live."

You can imagine, we were at rock bottom. For three weeks we were on the floor.

However, from the time Janet had her first mastectomy we went to the Pin Mill Healing Fellowship, based in Felixstowe, Suffolk, with its quiet laying-on of healing hands and prayer, none of the frantic noise, faintings and shoutings, crying, as at some places.

Both Janet and I received tremendous help from Esmond Jefferies and his willing volunteers, who made the Fellowship so wonderfully real.

Janet actually lived for 18 months, not two.

It was a miracle.

GREAT CENTRAL RAILWAY.

FINIS—DECEMBER 31st, 1922.

GENERAL CIRCULAR TO THE STAFF.

In sending you a circular announcing the amalgamation, as from 1st January next, of the Great Central Railway with other lines forming the London and North Eastern Group of Railways, it is fitting that I should take this opportunity of thanking you for all the willing and generous help you have given me during the past twenty-one years.

By no means the least of the assets to be taken over by the new organisation is the highly efficient staff of the Great Central, and those who follow me in the management of the line will be fortunate in having at their call the men who have helped so largely in making the Great Central Railway the effective transport agency that it is.

I hope and believe that the amalgamation—although the change of of name is a matter of regret to us all—and the enlarged company will be to the general advantage and tend to the well-being and happiness of the staff as a whole.

Finis – Grand Central Chairman Sam Fay's final message to staff on the eve of the 1923 railway grouping.

199

Bill
of Bulwell
by Bill Cross

This is the story of a Nottingham working man. As a child, Bill watched returned soldiers from the First World War live in poverty. He saw miners turned away from the pits each day after seeking work. He vowed he would never become a soldier or a miner. But he became both.

'Ordinary' Lives ❶

Series Editor: Ruth I. Johns

BILL OF BULWELL by Bill Cross. As a child, Bill watched returned soldiers from the First World War live in poverty. He saw miners turned away from the pits after seeking work. He vowed he would never become a soldier or a miner. But he became both. This Nottingham man's life story is now in its Second Edition. Available through bookstores, libraries or direct from the Publisher (£9.50 post free UK). ISBN 0 9516960 1 7

ALICE FROM TOOTING by Alice Mullen (1879-1977), including recollections of her daughter Bertha Mullen (1910-). Not many working class women of her time wrote their life story, but Alice did. It was discovered after her death. This book is "biography, local history, social history and a lot more," says the *Journal of Kent History*. It is a book "you cannot put down," says *Local History* magazine. Available through bookstores, libraries or direct from the Publisher (£8.95 post free UK). ISBN 0 9516960 4 1

Flo Child Migrant from Liverpool

by Flo Hickson

Placed in Barnardo's aged almost 5; sent two years later in 1928 (without her brother and sister) as a child migrant to the Fairbridge farm school in W. Australia: by mid-teens, Flo's fate was live-in domestic work...

Flo is a battler and made a life. But, revisiting Fairbridge in her 60's, brought her to a crisis point and she faced coming to terms with her harsh childhood, loss of family and country. Her life story, told with awesome honesty, illuminates the complexity of abuse and its survival.

'Ordinary' Lives **③**

Edited by Anne Bott

FLO: CHILD MIGRANT FROM LIVERPOOL by Flo Hickson has been welcomed both in the UK and Australia. It is the life story of a girl 'migrant' forced to leave her siblings and relatives, and to be sent to Australia, to suit the policies of Governments in order to populate the Colonies with 'good white stock'. Available through bookstores, libraries or direct from the Publisher (£9.95 post free UK. Post free Air Mail Australia, sterling equivalent of Aust $32.00). ISBN 0 9516960 3 3